THE CROSS TRUST

1943–1993

Sir Alexander Cross as a young man at Balliol College, Oxford.

THE
CROSS
TRUST
1943–1993

ENID GAULDIE

A TWENTIETH-CENTURY EXERCISE
IN BENEVOLENT PATERNALISM

Designed by Stevenson Graphics
Typeset and printed by Stevenson (Printers) Ltd., Dundee

CONTENTS

FOREWORD

As this monograph progressed toward completion it was suggested that it might be suitable were a photograph of Sir Alexander Cross to be included. The search, which was extensive and encompassed his many contacts and interests, proved fruitless until, as almost a last resort, his old college Balliol was approached.

As can be seen a very youthful Sir Alexander is portrayed. At first this might seem somewhat incongruous but then it could be argued that this was fitting taking in to account his subsequent interest in Scottish youth, and the continuing work of the Trust within this age group today. Considering again the difficulty in securing a photograph of Sir Alexander, even for those of us who knew him well, should not come as a surprise. He was an intensely private and sensitive person, one for whom self-publicity and flamboyance were entirely alien.

So it is that the present trustees deemed it fitting that recognition and record be made of the impact and place of the work of this trust within the canvas of our nation of Scotland. What is far more remarkable is to reflect the situation when Sir Alexander founded the trust in 1943. While others were in terror and striving to survive from day to day through the darkest days of World War II, Sir Alexander with courage and vision was able to raise his eyes to a brighter tomorrow with promise and opportunity for a younger generation and for those yet unborn. In a wide spectrum of fields and interests, from corporate to the individual, youth in Scotland were to have the opportunity to widen their horizons, and to learn to live life to the full in all its aspects.

There was always that twinkle in his eye as he introduced the somewhat naive young Scot to the delights of fine wine. It was all part of the process of getting to know people as individuals, and there are many Scots today who have contributed greatly to life in its many varied aspects who have reason to remember with gratitude the generosity of interest of this man.

It is now over 30 years since his death but those of us who have been entrusted to carry on this work started by Sir Alexander are constantly amazed at the variety of differing cases and problems with which we have to cope, and which he envisaged and for which he made provision within the terms of the constitution of the Trust. Today there have been great changes of financial and social circumstances but through Sir Alexander's foresight the trustees are enabled to cope. It could be said with justification that the work of the trust today is possibly even more relevant now than it was in 1943.

Great care and concern has been shown by individual trustees over the years. Indeed apart from one I have known all of them personally. The founder would have approved of their approach, he would have enjoyed their deliberations. He would not have approved of this monograph, at least in so far as his generosity and wisdom were at last recorded and recognised in the open! We are greatly indebted to Mrs Enid Gauldie for the time and sensitivity she has spent on producing this work. My old friend Anthony Ritchie, one who has contributed much in his wise approach to education and national life within Scotland, has with his usual meticulous care drawn all the strands together.

Mention too must be made of the sympathetic support of our secretaries Messrs McCash and Hunter of Perth. During all the years of its existence the trust has relied heavily on their advice, and in particular on James Ross and Mark Webster. One thing can be said with certainty and that is that all of us feel the more richly fulfilled from being able to continue this work. Our founder would have liked that, and then immediately looked forward to what the Trust should do in the next Millennium!

Robin D. Buchanan Smith

INTRODUCTION

This letter describes so well the rather special qualities of the Cross Trust and what it has done for countless young people that it will serve as the best possible introduction to the following history of the first fifty years of the work of the Trust.

The Cross Trust was of every importance to me. After National Service my name was put forward for an assistant conductor position with the then Scottish Orchestra but the directors decided there was no need for such a post and therefore my parents offered to pay for me to qualify in 4 years for a Company Secretary.

Music was too strong and through the influence of many famous musicians in Scotland at that time, I was advised to go to study opera on the continent, in Bonn. I was accepted as a volunteer student, unpaid, and a scholarship was needed to keep me. After being examined at the Royal Scottish Academy of Music and Drama by Henry Havergal and Wight Henderson I was recommended to Sir Alexander Cross. He paid me £450 and when my mentor in Germany suggested I needed another year he asked how much did I want?! I replied that I would be more than grateful for the same amount and Sir Alexander wrote and enclosed an extra £75 for me to return to Glasgow to visit my mother! After this scholarship I won the Philharmonia Orchestra Conductors' competition adjudicated by Klemperer, Boult and Giulini – best ever judges in a conductors' competition and my career was made. But without Sir Alexander's generosity I would be a very bad company secretary – if that!

He helped many of my colleagues as you will know – but such a Trust was very important to latent students who had already tried one path to a career and found it was not right. I shall forever be in his debt.

Yours sincerely,
James Loughran

1

THE BACKGROUND

The Scotland in which Alexander Cross grew up saw very dramatic changes in education. At the time of his birth in 1880 the Act which first provided compulsory elementary education was only eight years old and the system barely developed. When he was a young man at Balliol there were still many children as young as twelve working in the mills and attending half time schools. Then as an elderly man he saw the post Second World War developments which brought free secondary education and easily accessible university places for all.

Cross was not himself Scots educated, yet he set up a Trust exclusively for young people of Scottish birth which concerned itself during his lifetime almost entirely with Scottish schools and Scottish universities. He was plainly aware of a need to widen the horizons of Scots children and it would have been difficult for him to ignore the ravine which yawned between the privileged child and the deprived mill children, in schooling as in everything else. The extent to which he admired or criticised the Scottish education system is not easily gauged, but it is clear that he thought the pupils within it might benefit from his help.

There used to be a very widely held belief that Scots education was superior to England's. The basis of truth on which this rested was the existence in most areas of a school providing cheap education for all local children. John Knox's programme of godly training had laid down that there should be in every parish a school 'able at least to teach grammar and the latin tongue.' And in 1696 an Act of the Scots Parliament decreed the erection of such schools and their funding by the local heritors.

Thus many, if by no means all, Scots boys, though not their sisters, of the seventeenth and eighteenth centuries did have access to a reasonably good education not so readily available to their peers in England where all schools were either profit making or funded by charity and therefore very variable in quality. In the Scottish burghs education at a level above the primary was provided for the middle classes by the town council academies. Perth's was the first in 1761, followed by Dundee in 1786, Inverness in 1787, Elgin in 1791 and Ayr in 1794. The Andersonian Institute 'for the education of young gentlemen designed for manufacture or commerce' was established in Glasgow in 1796 and Edinburgh Academy in 1824.

At University level Scotland remained better provided for than most of England until after the Second World War. Scotland had five universities at a time when England had only Oxford and Cambridge. St Andrews, Glasgow and Aberdeen Universities were pre-Reformation foundations, with Edinburgh and Marischal College only slightly later. This meant that university education seemed a less distant possibility to children at Scottish village schools. It might be available only for the minority but for the brightest and best it was not utterly out of reach.

But, by the nineteenth century, when the rapid growth of towns had broken down the old social system and the opportunities for children to earn wages in the mills made their parents less willing to send them to school, it is doubtful whether Scots education had so much to recommend it. For instance, in Glasgow in 1868, of 98,767 children of school age, only 35,565 attended any kind of school.

In the second half of the nineteenth century concern for Britain's slipping economic position in the world drove some reformers to press the need for an educated work force to man competitive industries. Fear that France and Germany could call upon more technically competent labour to work in their factories spurred thought about the shortcomings of British elementary education. Worry about social unrest made the moral education and discipline of children seem urgent.

Scotland had liked to believe that its system of education had resulted in a widespread love of learning throughout all classes and a democratic society in which there was a sense of equality between a literate working class and its social superiors. To any unprejudiced observer this was patently not the case in the nineteenth century with factory fodder widely distanced from the employer class in the cities and bothy men well segregated in the farm toons. The fact that there were individuals who won through to scholarship in these circumstances does not alter the general rule.

The Education Act of 1870, followed by the Education (Scotland) Act of 1872, set up the Scottish Education Department, made primary education compulsory and free for all and provided for the setting up of a school inspectorate. Even before this Act had begun its work, there was realisation that it was not enough, that the country needed not only a competent and literate work force but a better educated clerical and managerial class as well. In Scotland the new Education Department confidently set about the creation of a national system to include both primary and secondary education for all. It was acknowledged that secondary education was needed for a much wider section of the population than could be provided for by the old merchant schools and the few town academies.

Boarding school education became convenient for the privileged after the development of the railways in the second half of the nineteenth century. The major independent senior boarding schools, Loretto, St Leonards, Fettes, Glenalmond are all Victorian in origin. The last of these became the particular interest of Sir Alexander, partly, at least because of its proximity to his home in Perthshire. How far he gave it his support because he admired its particular aims and outlook and how far his funding of particular projects may indeed have influenced the direction of the school's development is not easy to tell. He certainly believed that boarding school gave a boy independence, made him able to stand on his own feet without emotional dependence on his parents, encouraged the manly virtues of bravery, courtesy, public spiritedness and made him into a gentleman.

Only a very tiny minority of Scottish school children, perhaps six per cent of the school age population, had the opportunity of boarding school education, but there were many more ready to avail themselves of school after the primary stage. The Balfour Act of 1902 authorised local authorities to provide secondary education although such provision was not enforced until after the First World War.

The recruiting officers of first the Boer War and then the 1914–18 War reported the existence of large numbers of boys who were illiterate or who had only a very rudimentary grasp of reading and writing. Many of the young officers of the First World War, themselves gently reared in separation from the poor and ignorant till then of their condition, were surprised and moved by the lack of education of their men and it was partly their aroused compassion that began the movement for educational reform which grew to some strength in the inter-war period. Perhaps it was his own war experience that first stirred Captain Cross's interest in the need for improved educational opportunity in Scotland.

The Education Act of 1918, known as the Fisher Act, enforced the school leaving age of 14, thus effectually abolishing half time education, and set up a system of administration with comprehensive education authorities, each under a professional Director of Education. Secondary education was not provided free but the schools were built and staffed by the local authorities who were required to provide 20 per cent of free places. By such means the brightest of children might win through the system to the universities but the government did not provide enough money to fulfil all the expectations. Schooling for many was still perfunctory and short.

Between the Wars necessary reforms in education were much discussed in parliament and in the newspapers. There was growing concern about the injustice of the system of secondary education which encouraged the academically gifted but excluded the vast majority. The Labour Government of 1924 encouraged the development of secondary education and the Education Act of 1936 enforced the provision of primary education up to eleven years of age with secondary provision compulsory up to fourteen and selective thereafter. But at the end of the 1930s there were still problems and inequalities in all areas of Scottish education.

It was in this climate that Sir Alexander must have been contemplating how he could best use his money to benefit Scottish children during their education. His life had run parallel with a path of revolutionary change in ideas about education. There were still many and obvious gaps to be filled and he cannot have been unaffected in his thinking and in his plans by the philosophies developing and actively propagated during his lifetime.

2

SIR ALEXANDER CROSS

Sir Alexander Cross was born in 1880, the son of Sir Alexander Cross and grandson of William Cross, who was senior partner of Alexander Cross and Sons, seed merchants and chemical manufacturers, of Glasgow. The firm was already an old established horticultural and agricultural seed supplier when William took it over from his father. It expanded into chemicals and William's son Alexander became director in a number of industrial concerns. Born in Glasgow in 1847 and educated at Glasgow University, he married, first, Jessie, the younger daughter of Sir Peter Coats of Auchendrain, of the famous cotton spinning establishment and secondly, when his two sons by his first marriage were grown up, Agnes, younger daughter of J.G. Lawrie of the Glasgow shipbuilding firm. Thus an already prosperous old Glasgow firm was bolstered by connections with two extremely wealthy industrialists.

Alexander Cross was elected Liberal Member of Parliament for the Camlachie Division of Glasgow in 1890 and served his constituency until 1910. He was raised to the baronetcy in 1912. The family lived at 14 Woodlands Terrace, Glasgow and also had a property at Marchbank Wood, Beattock, in Dumfriesshire. There were two sons. The first, William Coats Cross, was educated at Rugby and took up a career in the army. He married an Australian landowner's daughter but had no children. His brother Alexander, the founder and first chairman of the Cross Trust, was differently educated, perhaps showing academic ability at an early age. He was sent not to Rugby but to Charterhouse and thereafter to Balliol. After graduating he went to London and studied to become a barrister and a member of the Inner Temple.

Alexander Cross was 34 years old at the beginning of the First World War. He served with the Glasgow Yeomanry in Palestine and left the army with his hearing severely impaired. A great many of those who survived that war emerged not only physically but emotionally damaged, some of them fortunate enough to find afterwards a role and a companion, some of them feeling unable either to marry or to be part of ordinary life again. Without his hearing Cross found that he could not continue his career in the Inner Temple and he did not work as a barrister again after the War. He returned to his native Scotland and, in 1925, first rented, and, later bought and settled into the comfortable house of Battleby, near Perth, and remained a bachelor until his death at the age of 83.

He did not entirely withdraw from public life but became a director of Scottish Agricultural Industries, an active benefactor of the arts and a very keen gardener. His main reason for his choice of Battleby as a place to live was that the garden would give him scope for his creative interest in plants. He maintained his connection with the family seed company and imported exotic and unusual plants through them. The garden developed into a show-piece, beautifully laid out, with many interesting specimens and of absorbing interest for other gardeners. His death in his sleep on 12 May 1963 occurred only a few hours before the planned opening of his garden to the public in aid of the National Trust for Scotland. His executors decided to open the gardens 'since it was felt that this would have been the wish of Sir Alexander, a generous benefactor who had on many occasions opened his gardens to the public.'

Major William Cross, the elder brother, died in 1947 and Alexander then became the third baronet. He found himself alone in the world with a great deal of money at his disposal, an administrative ability not being sufficiently used and a warm benevolence towards young people which he had no means of channelling.

Like many such men of his generation, isolated by circumstances from ordinary family life, he sought, consciously or unconsciously, an outlet for his own caring emotions which would be useful and per-haps valued by a wider community. There were, between the wars, many physicians, musicians and particularly teachers who gave their professional lives to the nurture and encouragement of young men. Cross's deafness made individual personal involvement difficult for him and he was, perhaps, diffident about the effect of a disfigurement received in a serious car accident on those who did not know him. But he had money and he planned to use it in a way which would both give a channel for his own paternal instincts and benefit young people in a genuinely useful way and at the same time keep him in touch with the young and their education.

The wish to do some good with one's money is not wholly unusual.

Rich nineteenth century manufacturers were prone, whether or not in an attempt to modify the dire effects of their money making upon the society they lived in, to give large sums for the building of hospitals, the laying out of parks and, sometimes, the alleviation of poverty. But they did prefer the poor to be deserving, that is docile, respectful, hard working. The unusual thing about Sir Alexander is that he seems to have been happy to help the not particularly deserving, to give willingly something a little more than was absolutely necessary to keep body and soul together. One of the characteristics of the Cross Trust was the immediately established tradition that those who were to be considered as beneficiaries should travel to Battleby, at Cross's expense, to spend a weekend with the Chairman. There is no known instance of his turning an applicant down because of his failure to fit the pattern of behaviour expected on these visits. Cross was quite sharp in his reports about some boys but always remarkably tolerant of youthful gaucherie. He was committed to the idea that his money, properly applied and at the right time in a boy's life, could help an awkward youth to emerge into a successful and acceptable member of society. And he was often proved right.

If he failed to reach the absolutely necessitous, if his money usually went to help the not very impoverished, that was not so much that he rejected the genuinely poverty stricken, more that their needs were not represented to him. There is, in fact, no mention of the poor or of poverty anywhere in the statement of the aims and proposals of the Cross Trust.

There could be more than one reason for this. Since World War I, nothing in Cross's life had brought him up against real poverty. His circumstances, living in the country, with a more than comfortable income, no extended family to widen his experience, made it possible, easy, for him to remain in ignorance of real deprivation.

Another, perhaps preferable, reason may be that he wanted very much to lift people above the purely material, to give them something more than just enough to live on, something to make life not just bearable but worthwhile. What he saw in Scotland, and wished to change, was spiritual poverty. There are plenty of instances within the records of the Trust of beneficiaries asking the bare minimum and being given a little more so that they could properly enjoy the opportunity before them. Cross wanted the lives of those he helped to be enhanced by his money and in many instances that did happen.

It was in any case his money. If he felt that he could do most good by rescuing middle class families down on their luck from penny pinching economies he had every right to do so. The same amounts of money, relatively small after all, could only have dropped into the ocean of homelessness and illness and hunger existing in Scotland at the beginning of the Forties. Spent as he chose to spend it, on individual young people with potential, it certainly did result in improvement in the lives of some of those individuals and may have spread wider ripples as those young people grew up to give their lives to medicine, music, science and learning.

Charity is not the most clearly motivated of human activities. For those without children of their own the wish to be recognised by posterity seems strong. For those with a passionate interest in any particular field the understanding of what money could do within that field, is powerful. Perhaps many rich people experience a vague wish to have their money work usefully after they have gone, to exercise power over its use as they did during their lives. But Government also provided a very powerful motivation when it introduced surtax.

The need to raise money to pursue the War and to reconstruct a war shattered country caused the imposition of tax at over 90 per cent of income for those in the super rich category. Few found this easy to swallow and for those opposed to the whole principle of the Welfare State it was hard to have so large a part of income taken away for its planned creation. Even if individuals subject to such rates of tax did not object, their accountants certainly did and the accountancy profession set about devising for its clients means of escape, if not from the tax, at least from the irritation of its going to government use.

Cross's financial advisers made plain to him that by allocating a large part of his capital to charitable purposes he could give away something like £200,000 without materially altering his own way of life. It must have seemed only sensible to set up a Trust that would use the income from that sum in a way that he himself found acceptable and which would at the same time provide him, as Chairman for life of the new Trust, with an interest and occupation in his retirement.

To say that the financing of the Trust was in Cross's own interest is in no way to devalue what he did. If it is not too clear how lively had been his interest in educational matters before 1943 he certainly did become interested and indeed enthusiastic about it once he had given it his attention, as witness the conferring upon him by St Andrews University in 1954 of the honorary degree of LL D in recognition of his service to education. His wish to give young people something extra, to open new doors for them, is plainly real and can be seen both in the stated intentions of the Trust and in the interventions he made in its administration over the years. His suggestions in the shape of little notes to the other Trustees, were always on the side of generosity and this was a tradition carried on by his successors as chairmen of the Trust.

Sir Alexander Cross was an autocrat, with the natural authority conferred by a good brain and a personal fortune, but in his dealings both with young people and with adults he does seem to have inspired affection. One is led to guess at different kinds of relationship with different kinds of people by the rather different ways in which they addressed him. To his cousin he was Alex, to Peddie, always Dear Cross, to Alick Buchanan Smith, Dear Sir Alex, and to some other correspondents, Sir Sandie. Perhaps this only reflects a complex and many faceted but generally benevolent character.

3

THE CONSTITUTION

The stated objects of the Cross Trust as expressed at its Constitution, were 'to provide such opportunities as may seem to [the trustees] fitting whereby young men and/or women of Scottish birth or parentage may be enabled to extend the boundaries of their knowledge of human life and to employ their leisure in such pursuits as will foster their love of nature and improve their physical health and well being; and whereby the British and especially the Scottish public may be participators in that enjoyment of drama and opera from which Captain Cross in his own lifetime derived lasting pleasure; and in particular, but without prejudice to such other objects of a like kind as may seem to the Trustees from time to time desirable, (a) to award scholarships, supplements to scholarships or other financial aid as set forth in Schedule A hereto; (b) to make grants for the promotion among the youth of Scotland of a love of nature and Scottish scenery as set forth in Schedule B hereto; and (c) to make grants to assist the performance anywhere in Great Britain, but especially in Scotland, in accordance with Schedule C hereto of such dramatic and operatic works and other entertainments as may seem to the Trustees worthy of support, the Trustees to give consideration in particular to plays by Shakespeare and Operas by Gilbert and Sullivan.'

The scholarships and grants referred to as set forth in Schedule A were for the purpose of allowing graduates of Scottish Universities or holders of Diplomas of Central Institutions (which then included the art and music Colleges of Scotland) and secondary school pupils of the United Kingdom to go to Oxford and Cambridge or any other university in Europe and also to a Scottish University: to a Technical Institute, Medical School, School of Music or Art within the United Kingdom or Europe, to any country in Europe to study its language and civilisation, or to a university in the United States of America or the Dominions'.

It is clear that, while educational grants were envisaged from the beginning, they did not come first in Captain Cross's set of priorities for Trust money. In fact it is particularly stated that the grants and scholarships should be awarded 'without prejudice to such other objects of a like kind' that is of a kind with music, drama and the love of nature. The emphasis is on opportunity, horizon widening, leisure well spent in health giving or cultural pursuits.

By their very nature these objects were harder to achieve because they could only be vaguely defined and because they necessarily involved value judgments. It was harder for the Trustees to decide whether a particular project in the arts, for instance, was of value than it was for them to take up references from headmasters recommending assistance for university places. And it was also more difficult for applicants to find the words to recommend their hopes and aspirations to the Trustees. It is not difficult to claim that any course of study might, if undertaken in the right spirit, 'extend the boundaries of their knowledge of human life.' On the other hand to claim that any particular project was of more value than another in improving their well being was more difficult. This vagueness was bound to make problems for the Trustees in deciding how best to use the funds at their disposal, not, perhaps, at first, when the Trust was little known and the number of applicants manageable, but certainly in later years as applicants learnt that the Cross Trust was more flexible in its aims and objects than some of the other grant giving bodies. There were occasions in the future when, in terms of the powers given to the Trustees under the Constitution, alterations were made to the Schedules, in particular Schedule 'A'.

Another point of interest is that Cross does not at first seem to have envisaged helping parents to pay fees at boarding schools and yet a very large number of grants during his lifetime was given for this purpose. Paragraph 6 specifically refers to young men and women, not to school children. Schedule A refers to graduates and to pupils who have completed or are about to complete their school careers. One must suppose that the application of Cross Trust money to the payment of boarding school fees came about because of Cross's interest in boarding schools, particularly Trinity College Glenalmond, which was so very close to his chosen home at Battleby. At any rate there was a perceived need and the constitution was flexible enough to make it possible to cater for it. Cross did not originally expect those who served in the management of his Trust to be out of pocket.

Powers were given in the Constitution for the Trustees to meet 'as and when they think fit', to decide what should constitute a quorum, to delegate tasks to individuals and to elect a chairman 'for the period of his life'. This office for life gave the chairman a firm grip on the Trust's affairs particularly as he had a right to a casting as well as to a deliberative vote if the Trustees failed to reach a majority decision. In practice, during his lifetime, this made it possible for Cross to conduct the Trust, which was after all his creation and his idea, as he pleased, rewarding any applicant who caught his fancy without too much regard to whether he fitted the terms of the constitution. The other Trustees might, perhaps, on occasions, refer wryly to 'Sir Alex's protégé' but they did not counter him.

It was not so much that it was difficult to argue with Sir Alexander, more that it was useless. In his own words 'I've noticed that my Co-Trustees, by way of airing their humour, when I propose any one for a grant, at once raise every kind of question and objection they can think of to his worthiness, without ever having the faintest intention seriously of turning him down – it is merely a little playful pastime with them.'

4

THE FORTIES

To begin any enterprise in wartime required great optimism. The war effort took all the nation's energy, everyone was tired, there was little surplus for initiative and imagination. Everyone was 'just managing', coping with the difficulties and restricted opportunities of wartime living. Even the rich were affected by fuel cuts, food and clothes rationing and the lack of imported goods.

It is fairly plain that Captain Cross was aware that his new Trust could not immediately move into effective action. Perhaps its creation arose partly from the need experienced at that time by many men of his age, who had experienced service in the First World War and were now too old for active participation, to do something that felt useful. To make plans for the future, even to contemplate post-war reconstruction, seemed important and worthwhile. And his wish to provide a little extra, a bonus for young lives, was strengthened by the drab, restricted, narrow lives most people at home were leading.

At the very first meeting of the Trust, held at Battleby House on 17 October 1943, the limitations of wartime were very evident and 'it was agreed that it was impracticable to make any awards or grants meantime under Schedule A,' that is under the section of the constitution which provided for the award of educational grants and scholarships. The impracticality seemed at the time to need no explanation but perhaps now, half a century later, it is necessary to explain that most of those who would have been judged by Cross to be suitable beneficiaries were engaged in war service. With all fit young men who were not in reserved categories called up at 18, university classes were very small and attended only by women and the few men who were excused conscription because of poor health or infirmity. Research work was almost at a standstill because so few of the post-graduate age group were free to pursue it. There were very few young men available to apply for the awards

The very first applicant was a young man still in the armed services who was fortunate enough to hear about the setting up of the Cross

Trust and sensible enough to put in an application very promptly in the Spring of 1945. Robert Howie, interviewed in June of that year said that 'he proposed as soon as he is released from War Service at the Admiralty to resume his studies in Politics, Philosophy and Economics at Magdalen College, Oxford'. It was agreed to award him £300 annually, paid quarterly in advance, as soon as he took up his studies again. In February 1946 Howie wrote expressing his very deep gratitude to the Trust 'for the generous amount of the Grant and also for the latitude allowed him in the matter of the date of his taking up residence at Oxford.'

The only other individual beneficiary in that period was Martin Milligan, a blind student, who was awarded a grant to pay for a reader to assist him at Oxford. Milligan was frowned upon by Dr Peddie because of a certain recklessness of manner which led him to run helter-skelter down College stairs, to show he could compete with the sighted and because of a certain suspicion that he spent his grant not on a reader but on more convivial pursuits.

It was perhaps not a bad thing that there was little pressure for grants from individual applicants during these early years when a very large number of the kind of young people Cross had imagined helping were otherwise occupied, 'extending the boundaries of their know-ledge of human life' in the armed services. It must have been dis-appointing for the Trustees but they set about the business of putting the Trust on a sound financial footing so that when the restrictions were eventually lifted, which, even in the dark days of 1943 they seemed not to doubt would come about, they would be in a position to provide real help where it was needed.

Awards under Schedule C, which would have provided grants for opera, concerts and theatres, suffered a different kind of restriction. Captain Cross took an interest in Perth Repertory Theatre and tried to discover what kind of help they needed. The need was clear enough. Everything, scenery, costumes, lighting, was run down and dilapid-ated. But it seemed that canvas and paint for new scenery could not be obtained. Such things were required for the war effort, for tents and tarpaulins and to camouflage tanks.

Costumes could not be renewed because of the shortage of mater-ials, even sewing thread, and the lack of clothing coupons. Every other theatre, concert hall and amateur dramatic company in the country was experiencing the same kind of restriction. At the second meeting of the Trust, on 20 May 1944, it was agreed that 'owing to difficulties in War time of effecting improvements in halls and lighting it did not seem probable that the Trustees would contemplate such grants in the meantime.' The Trustees were never willing to allow grants for unspecified purposes and the most obvious needs of theatre and concert directors could not then be filled.

Only under Schedule B, which awarded grants to youth hostels and outdoor activities was it possible to be of immediate help. Lord Keith, who always took a keen interest in the Scottish Youth Hostel Association, arranged for the purchase and delivery of two AGA cookers for use in the SYHA hostels at Carn Dearg, Gairloch and at Perth and for the provision of 250 fibre mattresses and blankets to hostels throughout Scotland.

The first Trustees, appointed as Captain Cross's own choice were Captain, later Lord, Walter Ian Reid Fraser, who was Cross's cousin as well as a fellow officer, the Honourable Lord Keith, a law lord, Doctor John Ronald Peddie, Secretary of the Carnegie Trust for the Universities of Scotland, and Colonel Hugh Baird Spens, of Maclay, Murray and Spens, Cross's law firm in Glasgow. Cross was to be Chairman during his life and the Trustees were appointed until their death or resignation. The number of Trustees was limited to not less than five and not more than seven but should a vacancy occur it was laid down that another Trustee should be co-opted as soon as possible.

At the beginning, and simply to provide an income for the purposes of setting up the Trust, Captain Cross provided an annuity of £1,000. The annuity was expressed in the usual terms, that it should be paid after deduction of Income Tax which had the consequence that the actual payment to the Trust by Captain Cross was for £500, Income Tax being payable at 50p in the Pound. However, a special benefit of charitable trusts is that they may apply to the Inland Revenue so that any tax paid on income received by the Trust could be reclaimed. Although the tax benefits for charities are still very beneficial it can readily be seen just how beneficial it was to the newly formed Cross Trust by doubling the initial payment of £500 to £1,000.

One of the expenses for which provision was made in the Constitution was the payment to each Trustee of a 'half-yearly fee at the rate of One Hundred Guineas per annum, unless he agrees expressly in writing to forego such fee for any year'. Initially, after the foundation of the Trust, it became apparent that the sum of One Hundred Guineas yearly to Trustees, even allowing for the Tax repayment would leave too little money for grant making purposes and Captain

Cross made it clear to his fellow Trustees that, at least for the time being, he expected them to forego their fees.

All charitable Trusts require to exercise care in applying their funds for suitable purposes; in particular if they are to obtain the considerable benefit of reclaiming tax on their annual income they have to satisfy the Inland Revenue that the distribution of their funds has indeed been for charitable purposes. The Cross Trustees with the benefit of no fewer than three practising lawyers among their original number, were clearly very well aware of the requirements but it also meant that they had the expertise in particular circumstances to advise organisations, to whom they might wish to give funds, of the benefits of obtaining charitable status. For instance, when Captain Cross first discussed with Miss Marjorie Dence, with whom the Trust was eventually to have a long and helpful relationship, how he could best be of help to Perth Repertory Theatre Company, it turned out that the Company was not registered as a charity. That meant that the Cross Trust could not reclaim tax on any funds paid to her for use by her company. The Trustees were, therefore, instrumental in advising Miss Dence how she should set about applying to be accepted as a charity and how she could benefit from that status in the future. In ways like this, not only with money but with expertise and advice, the Trustees under Cross's guidance were able to help a number of institutions, from outdoor training schools to youth orchestras, from choirs to exploration societies, from language courses to botanical expeditions.

As wartime restrictions ended, the existence of the Trust began to be known and the applications began to flood in, there was immediate need for more income. In May 1946 the Trustees noted in their minute 'the gift by the Chairman and purchase by him in their names for the purposes of the Trust of the following investments,' amounting on that occasion to about £80,000. Further gifts and purchases followed over succeeding years to the tune of something over £200,000.

Many of these shares were in South American companies and the administration and realisation of the funds sometimes proved difficult for the lawyers and accountants responsible for handling them, although they usually turned out to have been satisfactory, long sighted investments. Cross was not one of those who left the handling of his money to his brokers but had always been interested in its investment and involved with the choice of companies and their progress. Among those made over to the Trust in 1946 were companies like the Central Argentine Railway Company, the City of San Paolo Improvements

Company and many others which had taken his fancy and which proved to have been wise choices although they required some watchfulness and diligence on the part of those he instructed. Fortunately, when any delay in realising shares occurred he was always in a position to make a temporary loan from the Alexander Cross Seed Company Limited of funds to tide over the gap.

The end of the War brought many uses for Cross Trust money. One of the most immediately noticeable effects was the opening up of continental travel and the determination by the language professors of the Scottish Universities that their students should benefit from it. At the meeting held at Battleby in February 1946 Dr Peddie announced that there was to be a summer school held at Zurich that year and it was agreed that it would be a 'suitable cause to allow worthy but necessitous students to take advantage of it.' It must be difficult for young people of today, for most of whom foreign travel is commonplace, to understand the exhilaration and excitement of students in 1946 who had been confined to our own shores for so long and with no hope of travel abroad, who at last had an opportunity like this to travel across a devastated and long cut-off continent to Zurich and to stay there in the company of other students, absorbing the atmosphere of a foreign country, eating foreign food after years of routine rationed food at home, and hearing spoken the language they had learned only from books.

For those who travelled, not to the comparative luxury of Switzerland but to what had been Nazi occupied Europe or the defeated German state, things were more difficult if no less exciting. A student attending a summer school in Bonn in 1949 had to have special arrangements made by the Foreign Office to have British rations supplied to her by the Control Commission. Germany had nothing left for travelling students.

Letters received from these students afterwards expressed their gratitude for the opportunity and one of them suggested that his attendance at summer language school had played an important part in gaining him a first class honours degree and a university lecturing post.

After the October 1946 meeting of the Trustees, held on this occasion not, as usually, at Battleby but in the North British Station Hotel in Edinburgh, those students who had been to Zurich were entertained to tea in the hotel by Lady Keith, Mrs Peddie, Mrs Fraser and the Trustees. The students gave a full account of their experience in Switzerland, the benefits they had derived and the expenses they had

26

incurred. Captain Cross explained that the Trust would be helped by their reports in assessing how best to help other students in the future. 'The students were afterwards entertained by the Trust to dinner in the Hotel and those of them who could not return home that evening were provided with rooms and breakfast in the Hotel.'

This hospitality was in keeping with Captain Cross's ideas about opening doors for young people into a cultivated society to which they might not otherwise have access. It cost the Trust £11.10s. for the travelling expenses of eleven students from various parts of Scotland to Edinburgh, plus £12.3s.3d. for hotel expenses in connection with that conference. The same sum which now might perhaps buy after-noon tea for two in a hotel of that class was enough to give tea to eleven students, five Trustees and three wives, dinner for all of them and overnight accommodation for some of them. If this figure seems small today, even after allowing for the effects of inflation, it must be remembered that, although the War was now over, its effects on the catering trade as on so many other aspects of British life, were not. Lobsters and champagne were still in very short supply, the one be-cause the seas around our coast were still mined, the other because the wine-growing districts of France had only just been released from enemy occupation. There were severe government restrictions on the price restaurants, however grand, could charge for dinner. These controls had been imposed in an attempt to ensure that expensive restaurants could not buy on the black market at exorbitant prices. If they could not charge diners too highly they could not afford to pay suppliers above the legitimate rates. So dinners were modest in the 1940s even in first class hotels and chefs were forced to be ingenious in their use of available ingredients. These were the days of snoek, whale meat and dried egg, any of which might appear on any menu in sur-prising guise.

More usually, Captain Cross entertained students who applied for grants at his home at Battleby, often for weekend visits. He liked to make a personal assessment of applicants, trusting his own judgment about their worth and it gave him pleasure to entertain them perhaps more lavishly than they were accustomed to and to introduce them to the delights of wine, not at that time so common an accompaniment to dinner in Scotland. But on this particular occasion most of the students were young ladies, in whose company he was less at ease, and he was sufficiently a Victorian in his attitudes to believe that it was more in keeping with propriety to entertain young ladies in a first class hotel in the company of the Trustees' wives than in his own home. At this period senior language students were almost bound to be female because during the preceding years in which they had been studying, men of their age had been at war. For the first few years of Trust history, then, a large number of beneficiaries were women.

That balance was to change very markedly. In May 1947, for instance, of 14 students awarded grants, only 4 were women. Of the men it was reported 'All these students have had their careers interrupted by the War and are dependent on Government Grants which come to an end as soon as they have finished their course at the University.'

It was natural that men who had themselves experienced the effects of war on their careers, like Cross and Fraser, should sympathise with and wish to help returning ex-servicemen. But the Trustees certainly shared an attitude which had been very general at the end of the 1914–18 war and which threatened to become entrenched again at the end of World War II, an attitude which held that women, permitted certain freedoms during the war, should return to their proper place in peacetime and in particular should not threaten the educational opportunities or the employment chances of men. It was minuted that the meeting of May 1946, when a new policy was drawn up concerning the giving of educational grants, that preference should be given to male applicants in future. This was Dr Peddie's suggestion but there were no demurrers.

By the end of the 1940s, then, the Cross Trust had established itself as a body to which a number of individuals and institutions could turn for help. The country had not yet emerged from the deprivation of the war years. People were still shabbily clad, monotonously if adequately fed. Houses and public buildings were in need of paint and repair. Europe was still destroyed and full of wandering refugees. But the spirit of hopefulness, of new beginnings, can be seen in the wide variety of applications received by the Trust.

In fact in these first years of the Trust's life it perhaps came nearer to helping the really poor than it did in later years and this was probably because a policy about how to choose beneficiaries had not yet been established. The names reaching Cross during the Forties came usually as a result of Dr Peddie's contact with the universities. Professors, especially language professors, eager as they were to put their students in touch with European culture after six years of deprivation, were quick to see the benefits of good relations with the Cross Trust. Equally, in the light of its stated aims, the Trust could not fail to admit

the desirability of foreign travel, especially for those who were un-
likely ever to experience it without help. The Universities had, before
the War, held funds for awarding scholarships for foreign travel but
these were now 'sadly insufficient for the purpose for which they were
founded.'

Scottish universities had many poor and needy students, as was
their tradition, and the professors chose from among their number
deserving cases whose university careers were being limited by their
poverty, not only because they could not afford to travel. For instance,
there was a ships' plater's son who had won a scholarship to Queen's
College, Oxford who, on Dr Peddie's very favourable report as to
Hunter's steadiness and application to his studies was granted £125
per annum.There was another boy whose father was a gas meter
maker earning £300 a year who had gained a first class degree in
English Literature at Edinburgh and a place at Lincoln College,
Oxford, whom Dr Peddie called 'a scholarly, rather nervous but
gentlemanly fellow . . . a case which might very fitly be aided by the
Cross Trust.' Another, who had been in the RAF throughout the war
and had been chosen by the Foreign Office as suitable for a Cambridge
place in Russian, would have been forced to turn down that opportunity without help from the Cross Trust. His father was a locomotive
driver with British Railways and quite unable to help with Cambridge
expenses. A girl who was studying chemistry at Edinburgh was
recommended by Dr Peddie for a supplementary grant 'although the
circumstances are not quite in our line' because she was the daughter
of a Kelty miner and finding it hard to manage on her grant.

Local authorities in Scotland, who had the power to grant or withhold
the new grants for university education were still at this time, and for
some years to come, unwilling to award grants for students at Oxford
or Cambridge taking the view that Scotland had universities of its own
and there was no need to pay the extra amount involved in sending
students south. To be fair to the local authorities the Scots tradition
had always been for students to attend their local universities but even
where students had gained scholarships to Oxford or Cambridge the
education committees were not willing to make up the difference in
living expenses involved in studying away from home. This was one
way in which the Cross Trust was often able to give invaluable help.

It was very necessary in these post-war years to give help to men
rather older than the usual students. For instance there was Peter
Simpson, who had been employed as a tailor before the war, had

served in the RAF and been taken prisoner by the Japanese in Java and forced to work on the Sumatran railway. After the war he went, in a debilitated state of health, to Dundee Art College but by 1949 had exhausted his prisoner of war savings and was unable to maintain himself. The small grant made to Mr Simpson at this time was more than justified by his subsequent career. After graduation he did not become a teacher but was engaged instead as a designer by Donald Brothers, Glamis Fabrics, of Dundee and led that firm into the first ranks of post-war textile design with a very highly regarded range of subtly coloured, interestingly woven, linen and woollen furnishing materials which won export orders for Britain at a time when exports were the country's most important priority. He went on to become a governor of his old college, to represent Scotland on the Design Council, to act as an external assessor for design examinations and in the end set up business in a distinguished firm of his own on the Isle of Bute.

However it was never the intention to help only the very needy. By contrast the Trust was very happy to foster Miss Veronica Bruce, a well-connected young lady quite unaccustomed to poverty but with a brightness and initiative which appealed to the Trustees and a scheme which accorded very closely with the founder's ideas about spreading throughout a wider community his own pleasure and delight in music and the arts. She proposed to take a programme of ballet performances by four dancers and a pianist to 'theatreless towns and large villages' in Scotland during November 1948 and was awarded £200 for her venture. Then in January 1949 she was granted another £230 'to enable her to meet the expenses of living in London of herself and three other members of the Cygnet Ballet Company at £4 each per week for eight weeks during essential training there by Madame Nordi.' In September of that same year Veronica was awarded another grant 'to enable her to train herself and Bob Pender, under the supervision of Mr Idzikowski, to perform 'Spectre de la Rose' during the Cygnet Ballet Company's tour in Scotland this autumn and to pay for costumes and Mr Idzikowski's fees, which she cannot otherwise defray, all necessary to stage this performance.' It was minuted that this further grant was made 'on the recommendation of the Chairman.' In 1950 a further application for a grant for material to make costumes for the Cygnet Ballet was turned down 'after discussion of the income tax difficulties.' Miss Bruce's company was not a charity for tax purposes. However much the Chairman wished to help her the other Trustees were forced to persuade him that such help was outwith their powers. We shall see later that a way was found of getting round this little difficulty.

An enterprising young lady, this, whose situation was very different from that of most Cross beneficiaries during the Forties. But it was clear that projects with a difference and young people with a bit of dash about them appealed to Captain, or, as he became on his brother's death in 1947, Sir Alexander Cross. He was willing to help the plodders but he was looking for a spark. One of those in whom he, rightly as it turned out, detected a spark worth fanning, was Iain Cuthbertson. Cuthbertson, now a well-known actor, was in 1949 studying Spanish at Aberdeen University. He had been awarded a grant of £20 by the Hispanic Council to enable him to attend a course at Santander University. The Cross Trust gave him another £45 on the recommendation of his tutor who reported that he was an exceptionally able and most promising student. For a boy of 19 even to contemplate a trip alone to Spain in 1949 showed courage and originality. It appears that he spent the money on a motor bike so that he could see rather more of the Spanish countryside than would otherwise have been possible.

Much later the Cross Trust heard from Cuthbertson again when he came to Perth as director of the Repertory Company there and they recorded their pleasure at his success.

When first planning the foundation of his Trust, Cross could not have foreseen the extent of the social changes which were about to stir Scottish society. As a result of, first, the Beveridge Report, published, like the Cross Trust Constitution, in 1943, which formed the basis of the future Welfare State, and, secondly, the Education Act of 1944, which for the first time provided free education for all, the whole basis of the established order was changed. Even the framers of the new education policy had not properly understood the extent of the pressure for university places which they were building. It had been imagined that a smallish number of bright children would emerge from the working classes to take their place, still in a minority, among the middle classes who had always benefited from further education. The idea that there were legions of children capable of entering academic life, hitherto held back only by the poverty of their parents, was simply not grasped until those children began to work their way through free schooling and into university entrance. And, alongside the growing number of working class children staying on at school after the compulsory leaving age, was a growing number of middle class girls. Very many fathers, perfectly able to finance their sons' education, had traditionally baulked at the notion of paying fees for their daughters 'who would only get married'. Free education for all changed that.

The end of the war brought also a flood of ex-servicemen into the universities, both as staff and as students. Some of them were the sons of manual workers and minor clerks who would have had little chance of further education before the war. Some of them were already students in 1939 and had been forced, or had chosen, to interrupt their university courses. The Government allowed early release for service-men who planned to go to university, special entry qualifications for those who had not previously acquired the requisite school leaving certificates and in some cases arranged shortened university courses to allow the taking of a degree in two years rather than in three. For many of them it was difficult to settle down to study although their maturity and breadth of experience often allowed them to outshine the students who had come straight from school to university. None of them were the kind gladly to accept advice about life from the Cross Trustees and on the whole those gentlemen were content to make the grants and withhold the homilies. It was the view of the nation as a whole that life should be made as pleasant as possible for men who had given six years of their lives to the defence of their country and the grants from the Trustees were given in that spirit. But their presence within the universities was, if stimulating, also unsettling. It put strains upon the administration of the Cross Trust as it did on the whole educational system which had to expand in a hurry, adapt to a more mature type of student and alter the curricula to fit different needs. Professor Forrester, for instance, of St Andrews University, explained in a letter to Dr Peddie that the abbreviated Service MA was in many ways an unsatisfactory proceeding and provided problems for his College 'and will continue to do so until we work out our service candidates.'

Life inside the ivory towers had been a leisurely paced affair during the war. Many of the professors and senior lecturers were elderly men staying on beyond normal retirement age because those who should have succeeded them were at war. They could not immediately leave the reins to younger men but had to supervise and adapt to the changing circumstances of peacetime.

For the Cross Trustees there was a need to be filled but it did not exactly fit the criteria laid down in the constitution and dealing with the men was not as simple as dealing with boys from school.

It was at this time that Dr Peddie began his long service as a counsellor to students based far from home, travelling regularly to Oxford, Cambridge and London not only to consult with tutors about academic progress but to note the circumstances of each student and where necessary to recommend further help. It is often from his reports that we can gather the most interesting information about the working of the Trust.

Sir Alexander regarded Peddie's help as of inestimable value to himself and to the operation of the Trust. Through his appointment as Secretary and Treasurer to the Carnegie Trust for the Universities of Scotland, Peddie had direct knowledge of many of the problems of the young people.

The pattern for the typical Cross Trust beneficiary was being set in the 1940s but within that pattern there were some variations which would not recur in later decades.

Language students were at first, and would continue to be, one of the main categories to be helped. It was obvious that a student of French language and literature who had never left her own country would benefit from a trip to Paris in exactly the ways Cross had laid down in his constitution as desirable.

The difference between these immediate post-war students and those of later generations was that they had held during their childhood not the faintest hope of foreign travel. Many of them came from the kind of homes where holidays of any kind were not thought of. It has to be remembered that holidays with pay for the employed classes were not introduced until just before the War. Before that a day, once a year, saved for all year and amounting only to a trip to the nearest seaside town was all that most families could anticipate. Even for the well-to-do holidays abroad were not so very common and had, in any case, been out of reach for a whole school generation.

For the staff of the language departments it was different. The opening up of Europe was emotional and full of hope for them. Air waves echoed with the popularly nostalgic song 'The last time I saw Paris'. It was natural that they should be eager to travel again themselves and anxious that their students should experience the civilising effect of travel as well as practising their studied language.

There arose some small difference of opinion about the best means of ensuring this. The Zurich summer school was enthusiastically adopted but, after the first students returned to make their reports, some doubts were raised about whether this was the best way to experience living abroad. For students with confidence, staying alone with a foreign family where English would hardly be heard or spoken, total immersion in the language was best. But for the less confident student the protective shelter of the organised summer school and the company of other British students was useful.

At the beginning of 1950 Sir Alexander himself decided to travel to Europe to see for himself what was being done for students in Paris, Strasbourg, Basle and Zurich, whether they were being hospitably received and whether they were being introduced, as he would have wished, to theatres, concerts, art galleries and museums. It was necessary to make a special application for French and Swiss currency of £100. The ordinary traveller was limited to a lesser amount under government restrictions designed to prevent sterling from flowing out of Britain. In each city Sir Alexander was escorted by one of his beneficiaries and he came home armed with information which would help the Trustees to determine the amount of grant required for students in future.

Sir Alexander's own interest in and knowledge of music meant that musical applicants were gladly and unquestioningly helped. One young woman who must certainly have felt that the Cross Trust had changed her life was Daisy McDonald. In 1949 she was working as a typist in the office of McCash and Hunter. The conductor of the Perth Choral Society encouraged her to apply to the Trust for help and himself wrote a letter in which he said 'In my opinion Miss McDonald is highly gifted musically and definitely misplaced in her present work'. Miss McDonald told the Trust that it was 'my ambition to become a top grade violinist and I should like to obtain a good position in an orchestra such as the BBC Scottish Orchestra'. Her father was a railway guard earning £6 per week. Her own job as a shorthand typist gave her £3.9s. a week. Out of this she was travelling to Dundee and paying for violin lessons and practising for four hours every day after work. She had been advised that she should enrol at the Royal Scottish Academy of Music in Glasgow but the fees, railway fares and lodgings were beyond the family's means. The Cross Trust took up her case and made it possible for her to attend for two years at the Academy and to qualify for a post as a professional violinist with the newly formed Scottish National Orchestra.

In later years many students of music benefited from help by the Cross Trust. Most of them, however, were young people who may have valued but certainly took for granted their right to a musical

34

education. Miss McDonald was freed by the Trust from an unfulfilled life behind the typewriter.

The suspicion does arise that at this time less enthusiasm was felt by the Trustees for students of the sciences. They were almost exclusively represented during the Forties by men recommended by Dr David Anderson of the Andersonian Institute in Glasgow with whom the Trustees developed over the years a perceptibly uncomfortable relationship. This arose chiefly from Anderson's wish, and repeated request, that a block grant from the Cross Trust should be allocated to him which would be divided up as he chose among his students. A letter from Dr Anderson in May 1950 shows that he had suffered a reprimand on this point. 'There is after all,' he admits, 'something to be said for a direct contact between the Trust and the recipient of a grant'. And the Chairman has underlined this in red before presenting it to the meeting and written neatly in the margin 'Very much so'. The whole philosophy of the Trust depended upon the belief in personal vetting of and continued contact with individual students and Sir Alexander did not intend to yield on this point. The matter arose again in subsequent years and was always resolved in the same way and with some firmness. Colonel Spens who was anxious that the Trust should share his belief that technology deserved encouragement did not differ from the other Trustees on this matter, 'I think,' he wrote 'that I was responsible for putting the Technical College and the Trust in touch. I personally have a strong view that the more technologists from here see things abroad the better. I am of course utterly opposed to a block grant, but I do not think that eight applicaions are really too many when one compares them with the number of applications from language students to go abroad during vacations.'

The naturalists were more popular. The constitution had referred particularly to fostering a love of nature and so botanists and zoologists slotted easily into the programme. Vernon Heywood was made a grant in 1947 to study the vegetation in Spain and in the next year was helped to buy a car to make a return trip more fruitful. One student was given a grant in 1950 to study small mammals on Fladda. Another was helped with an expedition to Southern Anatolia for the purposes of horticultural research. This was dear to Sir Alexander's heart. The family firm was still a horticultural seed company in which he continued to take an interest and the laying out and planting of his gardens at Battleby was a major preoccupation. Apparently this particular beneficiary showed his gratitude by bringing back some interesting new varieties for the Battleby gardens. The goodwill thus generated proved important when one of the Trustees pointed out that, Southern Anatolia being outside Europe, it was in fact *ultra vires* to fund a trip there when the constitution restricted travel to Europe, the British Dominions or exceptionally the United States of America.

Among the visual artists helped in these early years was Alexander Wilson Burns, recommended by Douglas P. Bliss, the Principal of Glasgow School of Art. Bliss wrote a very interesting letter about Burns which tells a good deal about the rather insular world of post-war Scotland and the kind of cultural deprivation which Cross so particularly wanted to help. 'While strict attendance at classes and the daily hard grind of the student were of fundamental importance' Bliss wrote, 'there were other aspects of studentship of which, owing to his circumstances, he was entirely ignorant. He has, apparently, never attended exhibitions of art or even been present at lectures and concerts. I believe that an essential part of a student's existence is the social and cultural advantage that can be got from visiting the Museums from time to time so that an intimate acquaintance with the great heritage of the World's Art should be his.

'We can teach students here just as well as they can at any of the London schools, but outside these schools, and easily accessible to them, are the great Museums and it is the stimulus that comes from contact with the actual Masterpieces themselves that so many of our students lack.'

Burns had never been to London before and was ecstatic about the prospect. He was invited to Battleby and wrote a positively fulsome letter of appreciation afterwards. Mr Bliss, he said, had suggested a stay of three weeks in London. 'There is so much to claim one's attention in the art line, above all the thought it would broaden my outlook which is a great asset . . . The Director gave me a travel guide to London which gives the whole gaumont' (he meant gamut) 'of art galleries and museums and the principle paintings.' The grateful humility of some of these early beneficiaries is very touching reading today.

A very different young man was Robert Taubmann. A first class Honours graduate in English Literature, he had studied from 1938–40 and then from 1946–48. Between 1940 and 1946 he served in India, Burma and Malaya, finally commanding a company of the Black Watch. In August 1948, on the recommendation of Professor Talbot Rice, he applied for a grant 'to go to Italy to study art, archaeology and the literature and language with a view to his career, possibly with a publishing firm.' The Trustees granted him £150 for a first year in Italy but the Chairman decided this should be raised to £250. In January 1950 it was minuted that Mr Taubmann had spent most of the year in Florence but had also visited Piedmont, Aosta, Turin, Genoa, Lerici, the central Italian cities, the coastal villages and Venice. He spent the winter studying in libraries in Edinburgh and planned to see Rome and Southern Italy to complete a thesis on *Trends in Renaissance Thought*. The Trustees granted him £200 for this purpose but Cross received a letter from Peddie which expressed some reservations: 'He is undoubtedly an attractive man' wrote Peddie, 'and I imagine that when he does get something down on paper it will be well worth while. He is a bit of a dreamer and not altogether too well supplied with the qualities of "push and go" that are necessary for life in this harsh world . . . I am inclined to think that, by October of this year, he ought to be getting a job and that, while Italy is mighty pleasant it might be wrong to lull him into what is a sense of false security.'

Perhaps Taubmann, like a lot of ex-servicemen, had been required to exert more than enough 'push and go' during his war service. The most noticeable difference between the Forties and succeeding decades was, of course, the number of demobilised men looking for help in their studies. The Trustees were not always sure how much indulgence to give to men who were, perhaps, convalescent psychologically even if they were physically fit.

On the whole the situation was competently dealt with and wisely met and may indeed have widened the Trustees' own horizons and contributed to the wisdom and experience which greeted applicants in the future.

Two things made the difference between the Cross Trust and other similar bodies and they were apparent from the beginning. The first was that the Trustees liked not only to fill a need but to provide the something extra that made life enjoyable. They often gave a little more than an applicant asked and this must surely be unusual among grant giving institutions. Or, especially in the case of travel grants, they would assess the sum required for study abroad a little more generously than tutors had done. They were, of course, severely limited during the first years by government restrictions on the amount of currency that could be taken out of the country but they contrived to be generous wherever possible. This did not mean that they could be easily taken advantage of. They were quite capable of cutting the amount asked if they thought it exorbitant or of refusing altogether to make a grant to someone they guessed was just looking for a holiday. But they were more benevolent than most.

The second and rather important difference between Cross and other trusts was that they maintained an interest in their beneficiaries, granting further help either with awards or with useful introductions and placements in post-university careers. Once a Cross beneficiary, always a Cross beneficiary. This was a characteristic which appeared in the early days, obviously in conformity with the founder's philosophy, and continued as we shall see, into succeeding decades.

5

THE FIFTIES

The Fifties was a decade of innocent hopefulness which affected the whole country and is discernible in the minutes of the Cross Trust. The hardships of clothes and food rationing, of import licences and building restrictions did not immediately disappear and the Korean War returned the nation to fear of renewed aggression. But soldiers who returned to the cities after the War noticed that there were no longer barefoot children in the streets and teachers noticed the improved health of their pupils. There was no return to the terrible unemployment of the Thirties. The government's programme of building reconstruction brought jobs throughout the country. Young architects believed wholeheartedly that well designed buildings and well planned cities could change society for the better. Doctors, not all at first enthusiastic about the National Health Service, began to appreciate a new ability to improve the health of the hitherto neglected uninsured poor. Farmers, encouraged to take in marginal land and to produce as much of the nation's food as possible, were active employers. On the continent of Europe, although displaced persons still wandered helplessly and cities lay wasted and desolate, the cafés and hotels were opening up to tourists. Paris, if not yet herself again, was recuperating. Students applied for, and were usually granted, funds to travel or to perform at the Edinburgh Festival.

But if students were stretching their imaginations they were still conforming unquestioningly to the pattern of behaviour and appearance expected of them by a very conventional establishment. The Cross Trustees took absolutely for granted the need for a young man at university to wear a proper suit, a collar and tie, and well-polished shoes and to have a dinner jacket ready for formal occasions. Where these things were noticed as absent, grants were made to fill the need.

For instance, in 1955, Dr Peddie, reporting from his travels between universities, noted that John Gilbert had shot up several inches since taking up his university place and his clothes were outgrown and out at elbow. He was really in need of new clothes to enable him to continue his studies. It is perhaps difficult now to realise how used people had become to making do and doing without. A whole generation of young people had grown up quite unused to having new clothes and accustomed, if not resigned, to hand-me-downs and general shabbiness. It is interesting that the Cross Trust, usually represented by Dr Peddie, saw it as a duty to educate young men in how they should appropriately be dressed for a professional or gentlemanly life. In this particular case an extra grant was made to John Gilbert for a new suit at an estimated £15, shoes at £5 and 'shirts etc.', the etc. probably covering underclothes, at another £5. The cost of 25 weeks in Halls of Residence in Oxford was £85 in 1955 and the sum of £15 for pocket money considered adequate.

In 1956 Dr Peddie reported again 'a rather painful story of penury'. He had found one of their beneficiaries struggling with genuine poverty, cold rooms, not enough to eat and worn out clothes. 'His father is a Bible reader i.e. a man who goes about preaching and is dependent entirely upon the alms he gets from the faithful.' The Cross Trust saw that this young man was clothed and fed while under their care.

One of the first delights of the 1950s was the series of reports which began to come in about the academic successes of the grantees of the Forties.

Michael Webster, for instance, about whom one is intrigued because of the number of amused references to 'Mike' in the correspondence, had been the recipient of a grant of £175 per annum from the Trust while studying at Christ Church, Oxford. In May 1950 he wrote to say that he had been appointed to an assistantship in English at Edinburgh University.

Ian Jack, who had received £200 a year while at Merton had, according to Dr Peddie, 'made excellent use of his opportunities' and now had a lectureship in English at Brasenose and Pembroke.

Alexander Cheyne who had been at Oriel with a yearly grant of £175 was appointed in 1950 to an assistant lectureship in History at Glasgow. The difference in the monetary value of awards reflects the fact that most of these grants were supplementing scholarships won by the candidates and considered, in accordance with Cross beliefs, insufficient for proper participation in university life.

Peter Davis, who had been funded for the horticultural research trip to Anatolia must have pleased Sir Alexander when he was rewarded with a Junior Fellowship at Edinburgh.

There were musicians, actors and painters among the early beneficiaries, as we have seen, but of course their abilities are harder
to assess and their career successes slower in coming. One notable
success is Annette Crosbie, now a very well-known actress, reported
as being the best student of her year at Bristol Old Vic Theatre School
in 1953/4, from whom a warm letter of appreciation has recently been
received. The Cross Trust supplemented her grant of £147 from
Edinburgh Education Authority with a further £75. It was often the
case that the Trust supplemented awards made by other institutions,
a practice which accorded well with their policy of making life a little
more than bearable, of encouraging aspiration above mere survival.

Kenneth Elliott, later to become a distinguished musicologist, was
awarded a grant for a very interesting project, collecting and recording
ancient music manuscripts from Scottish castles, in 1951.

But it is conspicuously among the graduates of Oxford colleges that
the Cross Trust first saw the results of its grant giving.

One reason for this is that, until the work of the Trust became
more widely known, and they were not all that anxious that it should
be too widely known, the most usual channel into its funds was on
recommendation from the professors of Scottish universities to Dr
Peddie. Naturally the professors chose the brightest students in their
classes for recommendation and, equally naturally, those were the
students who aimed at an academic career.

In that period students who gained first class honours in an arts subject at a Scottish university were advised to go to Oxford or Cambridge,
and most usually Oxford, to study for a further degree. Although
some good research work did come out of the Scottish universities
and professors worked, sometimes for a lifetime without publishing
very much, at their own research, there was neither a tradition of
nor the facility for advanced research in Scotland and the war, in
which professors had grown old at their posts, had not helped. This
position was to change in the succeeding decades when research of
great and recognised brilliance was to be pursued in Scotland. But,
for the Forties and Fifties, a place at Oxford was the goal of the most
academically gifted of Scottish students and the Cross Trust helped
some of them to achieve it.

The freezing of posts during the war and the encouragement of
further education after it meant that there were vacancies on the staffs
of every university in Britain. Bright students with Firsts could reasonably count on winning an academic appointment. This was a situation

which would last throughout the Fifties and Sixties and which made the work of the Cross Trust rewarding and useful. Those beneficiaries could have had no conception of how difficult it would become for students just as clever as themselves to gain university appointments in more recent times. But for the moment these privileged youths upgraded from prize-winning Scots student to Oxford graduate to lectureship without too much difficulty.

In the succeeding years some at least of these successful young men kept in touch with their benefactor. Sir Alexander wrote to them personally with encouragement for their futures, with questions about their progress and with a continuing interest in their development, always stressing the need to widen their interest beyond the strictly academic, always eager to hear of concerts, exhibitions, theatres they had visited. They wrote back, sometimes with amusing tales about each other, sometimes confessing their troubles, not always only financial, sometimes allowing themselves to boast a little to one who would always be interested. He was, of course, a source of funds, and one suspects that on occasions cheques were despatched from his private account without recourse to the Trust. But he was undoubtedly something more and perhaps something quite exceptional. A truly interested but not emotionally involved figure can be of great importance in a young man's life.

The letters and visits, for the young men were encouraged to visit Battleby when they could, and the reports from Dr Peddie who continued to visit them on his journeys even after they ceased to be beneficiaries, were, of course, of much value to Sir Alexander himself. They kept him in touch with young people, with their lives and their ideas. He was by now a man of 70, without family of his own and he was glad to be a part of the life of this wider family of beneficiaries.

Dr Witte, of Aberdeen University, wrote to him in 1952: 'I am returning the two letters from Ian Stewart, which you kindly passed on to me and which I read with great interest. He is a lively and likeable lad, a good mixer with a great capacity for enjoyment; as you say, his stay in Switzerland will do him a great deal of good. It is very good of you to let these youngsters write to you in this free and familiar style, as to a friend and father confessor. You certainly have a knack of gaining their confidence . . . and their confidences! I have always noticed that they tell you far more about their personal affairs and their escapades than they tell me . . .' He goes on to mention by name a number of his students, one who is 'rather gauche, and even unprepossessing, but very able and gifted, a genuine "lad o' pairts" from a poorish home', another who is 'in the nature of a long shot', two or three who are getting on very well, another who is 'forging ahead'. Then he says 'I hope it gives you some satisfaction to see these protégés of yours getting on in the academic world, and to reflect that without your help they would not be where they are.'

There is no doubt that it did give Sir Alexander great satisfaction. It could be said that it gave him, in fact, not only a new interest but a whole new career in his later life. One can tell with how much attention he studied each letter by the way he underlines in red the point which he wishes to draw to the attention of the Trustees or on which he means to expound in his replies. And one cannot fail to notice the obsessive way in which he corrects the handwriting of his correspondents, sometimes going over nearly every word in a letter in his own immaculate hand. It has to be said that, in spite of all the present-day political comment about a deterioration in handwriting, some of those students of the Forties and Fifties wrote with a pretty poor fist. Not only the students received this treatment; even Dr Peddie's letters were improved, loops being carefully added in another ink to every l and h. So the letters certainly did not pass unregarded.

Parents also appreciated Sir Alexander's interest in, as well as his funding of, their children. One father wrote, in May 1951, to Dr Peddie: 'My son David, who was introduced to Sir Alexander Cross through your good offices, has now returned from Göttingen, full of Mediaeval History and a great many other things, and has resumed his working in reading history at Oriel. Obviously his horizons have been considerably widened and we have had the additional privilege of making an acquaintance with Sir Alexander, whom we find altogether delightful. He is also exceedingly good at dealing with the beneficiaries of the Trust and I find my parental responsibilities lightened by his very evident and practical interest in my son.'

Correspondents of Sir Alexander began to form a network which was useful to him and them. Stewart Sanderson, for instance, writing in August 1951 after an invitation to Battleby, was encouraged by having someone with a view wider than the academic to whom to write. One suspects that he had been getting something less than encouragement from his tutors. 'As you suggest, small minded people are apt to feel that one study should not be confounded with another and certainly never with journalism.' And he went on to give news of other protégés. 'I was amused by your tale of Mike Webster and his supervisor. I know Mike fairly well, as we used often to meet at the flat of our friend Derry Jeffares, who has just left the English Department here to take up the Chair of English in Adelaide. Professor Jeffares' sister was married in Walton on Thames a fortnight ago and I saw Mike at the wedding, looking very fit and in excellent form.'

Alastair McDonald was one of the most valued correspondents and when in doubt about whether a new applicant was suitable would sometimes be consulted by Sir Alexander. He replied to such a query in 1951 and sent with it a present of 50 cigarettes which were still in short supply and welcome to a smoker, however rich. 'I shall try to tell you what I know about Dick McEwen. He is a very nice person, well known to myself and most of the Aberdonians here . . . He is not a Mike or a Gordon: he has not got the all embracing, all simplifying mental powers of the former or the serious, contemplative, yes, religious (in its wider sense) approach of the latter . . . Dick is intelligent and he has humour. I should not say he has the depth of either Mike or Gordon but I shall not pursue this comparison because the two prototypes are, after all, rare spirits . . . As a person he is friendly, pleasant, sociable, modest and well liked by us all. He is not given to riotous living, does not smoke, is interested in and has a very good knowledge of music.' Needless to say, Dick got the grant.

In the future, of course, this spreading network of friendly correspondents meant that the work of the Cross Trust gradually became more widely known. It was not, in future, entirely the responsibility of Dr Peddie who, according to one of the letter writers was 'looking tired', to find and to recommend suitable people to be awarded grants, although it was still part of his assumed duty to vet most applicants and to commend those he liked best to Sir Alexander. Those who had already benefited from Trust help in their own student days naturally, as they attained academic posts themselves, chose to suggest to the Cross Trust their own most deserving students, or those they thought might appeal to Sir Alexander because of some singularity in their character.

The students helped during the Fifties were not by any means all university academics. There was James Lockhart, a brilliant student of the organ, who was helped to study under the best organists here and in France. There was Robert Taylor, the bass baritone. There was Cameron Bannerman, the painter, who wrote enthusiastically to Sir Alexander in September 1951:

44

I hope by this time you have forgotten the 'March of the Clans' and that you are back to 'auld claes and parritch'. On reading your views and doubts as to my project I took the bull by the horns and crossed over with a bundle of canvasses to Paris.

I must say the Customs fellows were cheerfully helpful and I stayed long enough in Paris to get my work photographed and the prints posted by airmail to the possible client in the U.S.A.

The dealer in Paris was very impressed with the 'guts' in my work, in fact she said she couldn't believe such strength came from 'cold tea and haggis'. Anyway, Sir Alexander, they have decided to pay for the framing of my work and also the price of transit so that's fairly good. I was a bit vexed at your remark about the appearance of the writing paper – it was my fault, I'm afraid as I was gazing at the letter when I had just finished a painting and I soiled it with my hands.

I had some of my own drawings criticised by a well-known critic who says I am on the right path but need more of my own queer personality to throb through my work. I feel within myself I need another chance to fulfil my profound thoughts into paint. Am I too Hielan in asking the Cross Trust to give me another supplement to study in Paris? The new colours of the Rouaults, Bonnard, Kisling, are leaving us cold men of the North miles behind.

Cameron got his supplement, a £50 grant to study colour in Paris.

Veronica Bruce, the ballet dancer, also continued to apply for and be granted help at this period as she had already done in the Forties. Her company was awarded a grant to help with another tour of Scotland by the Cygnet Ballet Company but in September 1951 she was asked to meet the Chairman and Mr Fraser to discuss the future of her company. There was a difficulty, pointed out by Mr Fraser, that the Cygnet Ballet was not registered as a charity for tax purposes. One suspects that its takings were not such as to bring it into the tax bracket. But of course the Cross Trust could not then help it without suffering a reduction in its claim for repayment of income tax. This difficulty was surmounted by forming a company to be known as 'Intimate Productions Ltd.', the word intimate referring to the size of the audiences rather than the character of the ballet. The company was limited by guarantee to the administration of the Cygnet Ballet and Sir Alexander Cross was named as one of its directors.

This was one means by which Sir Alexander contrived to help causes which appealed to him even when his fellow trustees judged that they fell outside the power to help of the Cross Trust.

Sir Alexander certainly had a genuine interest in all the arts and the Edinburgh Festival became a central point in his year, an occasion when he often met friends and beneficiaries who shared his interests. Perhaps some of his co-trustees were more inclined to what they would undoubtedly have called the more practical side of life. Even Dr Peddie, who was himself very musical and was thought of as a man with breadth of interests, was not above using the word 'artistic' in a pejorative sense. Colonel Spens was prescient in seeing the need for Britain to move forward boldly into a new technological age and, bowing to his opinion, fairly strongly expressed, the Trustees sent students to the Continent to study textile dyeing, to visit paper mills, to study silicosis in the mining industry and metallurgy in industrial works in France and Germany.

This practice was formalised at the meeting held at Battleby in July 1952 when it was minuted that 'assistance be given to students undertaking research in engineering, chemistry and metallurgy.' Dr Anderson again pressed for a sum to be set aside by the Cross Trust which he could then allocate to students of his choice but 'It was felt by some of the Trustees that this was taking the form of a Block Grant' (the capital letters indicate how strongly they felt on the subject!) 'and that the Trust was being committed for an indefinite period to making awards which could not easily be terminated. It was decided that . . . all applications should be considered individually.'

Almost certainly Dr Anderson's continued pressing on this matter, the manner of his approach and his unwillingness to let the subject drop, annoyed most of the Trustees and perhaps played a part in ensuring that students of the Humanities continued to predominate in the lists of beneficiaries. Cross was an authoritative figure, an elderly man not accustomed to being harried and it was always advisable to approach him with circumspection. He would forgive awkwardness amounting to rudeness in a young person, although he would always notice it and advise an improvement, but he was not tolerant of what he thought impolite in a person of position. Anderson, for instance, was reprimanded, in a way that must have touched his own pride, for having incorrectly addressed Sir Alexander in a letter on one occasion.

Spens for the scientists, Peddie for the Oxford lads, Cross himself for the artists and musicians, the interests were shared among the Trustees. Lord Keith was the one who chose to emphasize that part of the constitution designed to encourage a love of nature and out-door activities. It was he who kept the Trust in touch with the Scottish

Youth Hostel Association and who regularly recommended grants to them for the building and furnishing of new youth hostels. Until the Fifties almost all hostels in Scotland had been old cottages, often with only the most basic amenities, outside lavatories, sluggish coal-fired ranges and oil lamps. Now the Association embarked on a programme of buying and converting larger properties and building new hostels and the Cross Trust made funds available, usually anonymously, for this enterprise.

The Moray Sailing School and the later Outward Bound adventure training schools which followed it also attracted interest and funding from the Cross Trust and it was probably the emphasis on outdoor sports, particularly of the non-competitive variety, mountain climbing, sailing and skiing, which enabled Rannoch School, newly founded in this decade, to win their support.

Most of the ex-service students had graduated by the mid-1950s although there were one or two who had embarked on particularly long courses or who, because of their importance in resettling a liberated Europe, had not been immediately released at the end of the war. It was suggested to the Cross Trustees that their declared and still adhered-to policy of favouring men, especially ex-servicemen, was becoming rather unfair to some women students, especially where, as in one case, it looked as if two extremely bright girls were going to be rejected for awards because they were in competition with two ex-servicemen of lesser ability. It was hardly the fault of these young women that they had been at school during the war and unable to serve their country.

A new problem presented itself during the Fifties. Although the war was over, conscription did not end and young men were obliged to do two years' National Service when they left school, unless they were destined for certain reserved occupations. While every sympathy had been given to wartime soldiers, these National Service men attracted less understanding. Many fathers, for instance, who would unquestioningly have accepted their responsibility for continuing to educate a boy as he moved on from school to university, baulked at the idea of maintaining an ex-serviceman in his twenties and only beginning his further education. There were many applications for help from men in this category and the Korean war's outbreak ensured that conscription would not quickly be abandoned.

Assistance with boarding school fees became common during this period although it seems neither to have been envisaged by the founder nor indeed allowed for in the original regulations of the Constitution (although the Trustees had power to alter those regulations). That the point was stretched to allow for the payment of fees in what were judged to be needy cases was due to two circumstances. One was the rising cost of running such establishments and bringing them into conformity with new government regulations about conditions in independent schools. This inevitably resulted in rising charges at a time when many families, whose incomes were not keeping pace with the rising cost of living, were having some difficulty in finding the fees. In some cases there was real hardship involved and a danger of a child being removed from a school environment in which he was happily settled.

The other circumstance was the proximity of Battleby to Glenalmond School. Sir Alexander Cross took on the role of benevolent neighbour to the school, valuing the friendship of the masters, especially of the music department and taking a kindly interest in the boys. Sometimes he took his weekend visitors over to meet the pupils. One such beneficiary, an ex-pupil of Loretto, wrote to say 'how very much I enjoyed the two days I spent with you at Battleby. It was a great pleasure to meet so many charming people at Glenalmond which I can hardly continue to regard as a hostile encampment.' Sir Alexander wrote to his cousin, Ian Fraser, in 1958, with obvious anticipatory pleasure: '"Commem" celebrations at Glenalmond tomorrow, which will keep me busy with sundry entertainments. Jock Macdonald and his Oriel pal, Duncan McNeill, come here this afternoon to join in the rejoicings. I took a car load of flowers over yesterday to four suppliants for such adornments.'

Both masters and boys were frequent visitors to the house and gardens of Battleby. Hospitality was provided and the gardens of Glenalmond revived and stocked with Sir Alexander's assistance. It was inevitable that hard cases should be brought to his attention both by this and other schools: the widow struggling to keep a son at school, the Polish ex-officer whose estates and wealth were left behind in Poland but who wanted a gentleman's education for his son, the company director whose firm had gone bankrupt, all found a sympathetic hearing. As the possibility of gaining help with school fees became better known there were more and more applications. Some of these were genuine cases of misfortune and hardship. Some of them, one can only say, seem now to have been less urgently in need. There are always degrees of poverty and one family's comfort can seem like penury to another. It was obviously difficult for Sir Alexander to reject appeals for help.

The trouble was that boys, once helped at a tender age, seemed to become the responsibility of the Trust for the rest of their lives. It was difficult to refuse a grant to go to Oxford to a boy whose fees had been paid at school, the circumstances of whose parents had not changed and who had worked hard to obtain a scholarship. Before long the Trustees had to accept the fact that there were too many long-term continuing grants, absorbing such a large proportion of the funds at their disposal that they were left with only sparse amounts to make new awards, however deserving the applicants.

Already by 1955 attention was drawn at the Trustees' meeting 'to the large number of recurring grants and consequently smaller amounts of money available for new grants in any one year.' At the same meeting the Chairman asked the Trustees to consider whether grants should be made 'to boys whose parents find difficulty in sending or keeping them at Scottish Public Schools or Glasgow or Edinburgh Academies.' No decision was made at that time about whether it was within the powers of the Trust to do this but at the February 1956 meeting it was decided that it was *intra vires* and a grant was made to a 13½ year old to attend Merchiston Castle.

When one case had been allowed, many followed and it would seem that the Trustees were never completely happy in their minds, or perhaps never completely in agreement, about the question of school fees. For the most part Sir Alexander seems to have found a way round the difficulty by helping people out of his own pocket. He set up a private fund, separate from the Cross Trust, from which he could personally help cases of hardship from Glenalmond without criticism from the other Trustees.

He also helped Glenalmond with expenditure on items which might otherwise have contributed towards a rise in fees. The Trust made a grant of £130 for costumes for a performance of Princess Ida, for instance. It spent £150 on 'a really good violin, bow and case', for a Glenalmond boy whose father could afford 'only a rather poor little violin' and later paid £350 for a new Steinway grand piano. They granted £30 for expenditure on Art books for Glenalmond library. It does seem that Sir Alexander was inclined to jump in and promise things to Glenalmond and to ask his co-Trustees for their opinion afterwards. This may at times have caused dissent if not open protest but the general consensus was that, in the final test, it was his money and his Trust and he had a right to do what he wanted with it. School fees, for Strathallan, Rannoch and Craigclowan as well as for Glenalmond continued to be paid when Sir Alexander thought a case warranted help. And in their future careers it certainly seems to emerge that Glenalmond boys had only to ask to be granted favours and help. At a very important meeting held in April 1961 to discuss the effect upon the work of the Trust of the Anderson Committee Report, it was agreed again that 'it would be reasonable to award part of the Trust funds to students proceeding to public schools where the government gives no assistance or only minor assistance.'

The rest of that report falls to be discussed in the next chapter but this particular decision, agreed when some much more pressing matters had to be decided, illustrates how strongly Cross felt about his right to help his friends and their children and how important those friends had become to him. While the other Trustees would, one guesses, have totally accepted the philosophy that sending a boy away from home to boarding school was good for him, the important thing for Cross was the support for his friends and for what had, in fact, become his family.

Among the boys in whom he took an interest while at Glenalmond was one to whom he took a particular liking and whose father became a close personal friend. Robin Buchanan Smith was awarded a grant to study history at Cambridge in 1954. As a result of Sir Alexander's meeting with his father, Sir Alick Buchanan Smith, later to become Lord Balerno, a firm friendship based on mutual liking and trust was struck up. This resulted in Sir Alick's appointment as a Cross Trustee on the death in 1956 of Colonel Hugh Spens. In 1959, when Robin Buchanan Smith graduated and took up an appointment as chaplain to St Andrews University, he too was invited to become one of the Trustees. His character and personality had appealed so much to Cross that he wanted him as a colleague.

The original Trustees were now elderly men. Cross himself was 79 and had suffered a severe attack of shingles from which he recovered only slowly. Students in Oxford noticed on his visits of inspection that Dr Peddie was looking tired. Ian, soon to be Lord, Fraser was increasingly occupied elsewhere. There was need for new and younger blood and it was unusually far-sighted of such a body to co-opt to their number someone so very much younger. Robin Buchanan Smith's election was an important one for the Trust. It brought a new and modern viewpoint to a group of men who, however much they struggled to be liberal-minded and to understand the post-war world were irretrievably men of the 1930s. Even more unusual was to co-opt Mr Buchanan Smith as well as his father, so that two generations of one family were to sit on the Trust, influencing its direction for the next stressful decades. For the Sixties were coming, the unsettling, overturning, revolutionary Sixties.

Of course perceived periods in history do not end neatly with the end of a calendar decade. Although this chapter is entitled The Fifties everything that characterised the Fifties flowed gently on into the first years of the Sixties. Since the tiredness and depression of post-war times, when the effects of the terrible poverty of the 1930s still made a dramatic divide in the nation, to the late 50s when slums had been cleared, modern housing built, full employment created, adequate health care and access to education provided, the nation had been transformed. Young people from every kind of home had developed high expectations of what was possible. They could study in Rome and Paris, they could explore the Atlas mountains, they could become painters and concert pianists and art-historians. Spiritually they aspired, while their material expectations remained low. Television and the rampant advertising profession had not yet raised the level of demand for what are now called consumer goods. Students, in fact, asked so little that Sir Alexander began to feel it necessary to instruct them in how a gentleman should dress and to provide funds to make sure that their wardrobes were correctly furnished. This is the period in which the 'kitting out allowance' was invented. Its purpose was partly to provide funds for families who were for one reason or another excluded from other forms of help. But it was also partly because of a perceived need to make sure that Cross beneficiaries looked like gentlemen.

The image of a gentleman was to undergo some revision in the following decade.

6

THE SIXTIES

In May 1963 Sir Alexander Cross died at the age of 83. The Trust which he had formed was now 20 years old and well established as a benefactor of Scottish youth and a supporter of Scottish culture. His passing was marked with great restraint, probably at his own wish, and at the meeting of the Trustees at 20 Moray Place, Edinburgh on 24 June the minute reads that 'The Trustees wish to put on record their admiration for his far-sightedness and imaginative generosity in founding and endowing the Cross Trust and their affectionate regard for him as their first Chairman.'

There would be no more convivial weekend meetings at Battleby. When the SYHA let it be known that they were contemplating the building of a new hostel at Aviemore the Trustees made a grant of £4,750 for the purpose and, agreeing that it would be a fitting memorial for Sir Alexander Cross, reserved the right to choose a name for it. In the event they decided not to give it a special name but to have a commemoration plaque erected inside the building.

Sir Alick Buchanan Smith was elected as Chairman. Of the other Trustees, Lord Keith was probably not well enough for any extra duties. He died in the following year. Ian Fraser was elevated to the Scottish bench in January 1964, and was more than fully occupied. Dr Peddie had already accepted an extra burden by agreeing to take on the personal vetting of all applications for grants. It would in some ways be easier for him to have more control over incoming applicants, without the founder's frequent suggestions of help for his own acquaintances and protégés, but it would also mean more work and more travelling. He had more than enough to do.

Sir Alick, who became Lord Balerno in September 1963, was quite differently experienced from his predecessor. He was a scientist, the son of an academic, one of a close family, with brothers and sons of his own, and a university lecturer. His knowledge of young people was based on real experience of them in his own home and as his own students. He had none of Cross's fanciful, whimsical delight in the very presence of young people around him. He was too used to it. But he did share Cross's benevolence and charitable understanding of them. It was probably easier for him to assess when to put his foot down, when was the moment for forgiveness and indulgence, when the moment for firmness and insistence upon respect. He was undoubtedly a clever, kind and a tolerant man, with a twinkling sense of humour. And the coming years would bring a need for all his tolerance.

The Sixties saw great changes in the attitudes of young people. Education could no longer be represented to them as a privilege. It had become a legal right. And with that assumption of right came the belief that self-sacrifice should not be required of a student as a condition of his access to education. Comfort and pleasure came to be expected and counted on rather than hoped for. A fairly blatant illustration of this came just before Cross's death when one applicant applied for a grant 'to provide for necessary furnishings, clothing, subscriptions to clubs and societies, travelling and other general expenses, occasional entertainment and vacation expenses during his first year at Oxford and also to allow him to contribute to the upkeep of his home.' His father was a Company Director, his mother had a private income from equity holdings paying high dividends. He had won a £100 scholarship, had an SED grant of £208 and the Trust awarded him another £100. He was a 'close personal friend of a cousin of our Chairman' and, as he had fairly carefully described exactly the kind of extra curricular activities which the Chairman had always recommended as an essential part of a university career, it was hard to refuse him. Two years later he applied for and was awarded £50 to study sculpture in Greece. It is quite difficult not to feel that during this period the Trust was providing help not so much for those who needed help as for those who knew how to set about getting it. There was a mixture of those desperately trying to find the means of educating themselves and those from comfortable middle class homes just trying to wangle a bit more.

The Trust did, however, hear about and give help to more genuinely needy cases. There was a young ballet student who had won a place at Sadlers Wells, whose father was a janitor and mother a cleaner, and who was found to be ill from malnourishment after trying to live in London with only £1 a week to spend on food. Lord Balerno discovered another student who was 'obviously undernourished and underclothed and clearly in need of a grant to purchase more adequate clothing and to supplement his present insufficient diet so that his health and morale may be maintained adequately to undertake his present severe course of study.'

But, with the advent of legislation which directed mandatory payment of further education fees and Scottish Education Department maintenance grants based on parents' income for all students, the kind of hardship which had once impoverished some students no longer threatened. The Trustees under Lord Balerno set about rationalising their policy about grant giving. The existence of state support freed them from any fear that rejection of an application might abandon young people to real poverty.

In the Sixties there were many more calls upon their income and because the state was already providing support for many of those they would once have helped, they turned down many more applications than they granted. One family, who had more or less lived at the expense of the Cross Trust during Sir Alexander's lifetime was interviewed and told that indulgence was coming to an end. A man of 40 who sounds like the proverbial perpetual student was told that he could not have a grant. Strathclyde University, successor to the Andersonian Institute, was firmly told that they could not count on obtaining as much assistance as they had had in the past. University language departments were told that if travel abroad was now a mandatory part of the course it should be paid for out of course fees.

On the other hand astonishing generosity is shown to some other applicants. In July 1964 a consultant physician seeking help was told 'The Cross Trustees are sympathetically disposed towards parents who are "too well off" to be able to afford to send their sons to the university.' Any parent who has been in the position of earning just too much to qualify for a grant for his children while seeing others only marginally less well paid enjoying state support will understand the dilemma here. The Trustees were not unaware that poverty is relative, that parents of this kind would not be experiencing real hardship but only giving up minor extravagances to pay for their children's education, that much more deserving cases existed. Where the more deserving cases came to their notice, they helped them. But they were men of their class and of their time: they could not help but see the point of view of their own kind. And where they did come face to face with people of another class they sometimes found it difficult to be benevolent without being condescending.

'The father is a decent enough chap, but with no education and a slight chip on his shoulder.'

'I saw this lass last Wednesday and found her a much more presentable person in manner and speech than her telephone mode of conversation had led me to expect. She seems to be a typical product of the Boroughmuir School.'

'At first sight he is a typical product of what you would expect from Oban High School. In fact he has an astonishing record of climbing and hiking through the hills.' This boy was applying for a grant to go on a British Schools Exploring Society Expedition and it was suggested that 'This is just what this young man requires to develop his self-reliance. Last February he took a party of 7 other boys from Taynuilt, Bridge of Orchy, Devil's Staircase, Mamore, Glen Nevis to Fort William in appalling weather conditions of snow and ice over four days.' This apparently was not self-reliance, and leadership could not be expected from Oban High!

The Trustees really did believe that boarding school was better, that it developed qualities that could not be developed in a boy living at home. Believing that, they can hardly be blamed for lending their support to those who fitted the pattern to which they themselves conformed. They tried to be, and indeed believed themselves to be, broad-minded but they could not prevent themselves, for instance, from finding regional accents either amusing or deplorable. 'She is an extremely attractive person' they said of one girl 'with a magnificent Glasgow accent.' 'The father' on another occasion 'is a stocky Scot who had retained his Ayrshire accent despite his sojourn in Malaysia.' And they did still believe in the need for a conventional appearance: 'He is a pleasant young man and his hair, though not as short as it should be, is not by modern standards very long.' A drama student was reported as 'having no suit and his shirts are far gone.'

It was plain that the manly virtues were admired and a gentlemanly bearing expected. While a character out of John Buchan seems to have been the desired role model, the Trustees are sometimes more motherly than anything else in their remarks. 'He struck me as a very competent, lusty schoolboy' read one report. Of another it was said 'I had him with me last night and was much impressed by how he has matured during the past year. He has grown up mentally as well as physically (now 6ft 2in tall).' One boy was said to have 'developed well from the insignificant but very bright small boy.' And another who had been 'Sir Sandie's protégé from Windsor' was said to be 'a very happy boy, enjoying games, coming on well as a piper. He is over 6ft tall and is still growing. I think Sir Sandie would have been more than satisfied with him.'

They were good men, trying hard to be adaptable to a world which was fast changing around them.

There were, during the 1960s, certain legal changes which affected the work of the Trust. Until this time Scots students whose parents could not finance their university courses had been helped by the Carnegie Trust for the Universities of Scotland. Where he found students who needed more help than Carnegie could give, Dr Peddie recommended grants from the Cross Trust. But, from 1962, Section 117 of the Education (Scotland) Act required registration with the Scottish Education Department of all educational charities. In fact the Cross Trust seems to have escaped notice until 1965 when, in the October of that year, the SED insisted on registration, asked for a constitution of the Trust and for a list of their investments, as they had the right to do.

It is likely that Sir Alexander Cross would have seen this as bureaucratic interference, however laudable the intentions of the Act. For his successors acceptance was inescapable. There were two immediately felt effects. The first was that thereafter every penny the Cross Trust gave to a student above a certain figure would simply be deducted from his or her SED grant, leaving him or her no better off. From now on the Trustees had to take care to give only as much as would not endanger the SED grant, finding other ways, where possible, to supplement it.

One of the ways chosen to circumvent the SED's harshness was the 'kitting out' grant, a one-off sum for a particular purpose which did not, apparently, infringe the rules but must have been of great benefit to many families. The device had been used before. Now it became an essential part of the Trust's policy. In September 1967 Robin Buchanan Smith reported about one needy boy: 'It is a wonder how his parents manage to keep up appearances. Gerald has been staying with me and he is still wearing for best the suit he had at school. I suggest that the simplest way would be for us to give him a grant of £100 to outfit himself properly.' And of another boy it was said 'This cheerful youth has to provide himself with a Dinner Jacket and appurtenances to keep up with the generality of Officer Cadets. He has not asked me if the Trust could help him in this, but I discern the need.'

This particular boy illustrates the fact that the Buchanan Smiths, father and son, carried on as far as they could the founder's tradition of entertaining boys for weekends in their own homes, but that, especially in the case of Robin Buchanan Smith, the boys were chosen, not so much for their musical interests or attractive manners as for their need. In this case the letter continued 'There is virtually no home for the lad. He hasn't seen his father for many years and he regards the House of Cockburn as the best under the circumstances.'

The second effect of the need for registration with the SED was that officials at the Department began to advise a great number of students to apply to the Cross Trust for financial assistance in carrying through their studies. Of course the Trust had in the past frequently made grants for postgraduate research but in more recent years, finding their funds inadequate to fill every call upon them, they had largely restricted themselves to helping undergraduates. The students who most often sought advice from the SED regarding funding were those who had failed exams and thus in order to continue their studies would require to repeat a year. Government grants were not available for this but understandably such applicants were not considered to be suitable beneficiaries of the Trust.

The matter was not easily resolved. Lord Balerno's university experience was of great benefit to the Trust at this time, partly because he was aware of other sources of funding available to research students and partly because of his ability to evaluate academic work. It was decided firmly that, as a general rule, the Trust would not subsidise thesis work, largely 'because so many students at various stages of their careers are engaged on theses that we would be swamped if we did.'

This illustrates the extent to which original research had become important within the university system. In the old Scottish universities, in which by far the greatest number of students were being educated for school teaching and where lecturing appointments were usually for life, research had been of less central importance. Now anyone hoping to pursue an academic career (and the rapid expansion of the universities both in number and size had encouraged bright students to aim in that direction), needed to have a list of published work behind him. The emphasis on originality meant that new subjects were sought with increasing urgency and articles published on ever more minor topics. There was something almost feverish about the output of research work from the universities at this time and every research student was looking for funding for his research. It was the beginning of the trend towards the present situation in which government bodies judge and fund universities on the quantity of the research work issuing from them.

At any rate it put considerable pressure on the funding bodies, and charitable trusts found themselves, as the Cross Trust had feared, swamped with applications for help. The decision was made in 1970 'to take the line that we may award these grants only to those beneficiaries of ours who have shown exceptional merit in their undergraduate careers.'

This was a reinforcement of the policy of continuing support for young people who had already been accepted by the Trust as suitable for help, had been helped often with school fees, travel grants and university funding and were now applicants for help as postgraduates. With so many applicants to choose from it was not unreasonable to continue to look after those already known to them, to 'keep their ain fish guts tae their ain sea maws' so to speak. It made it easier to judge whether the money would be well spent.

With so many of the traditional ways of judging respectability now scorned by the wider society, making decisions about who was most worthy of help became more and more difficult.

Women, as we have seen, were treated with some discrimination immediately after the war, just as they had been after the First World War. The excuse of making way for ex-servicemen could not last but its passing did not restore a balance of male to female beneficiaries. The idea died only slowly that, while women should have a right to education, they should be given their places only after all the qualified men had been accommodated. The figures for Cross Trust grantees reflect this. In 1957/8 all those given aid at Oxford and Cambridge and at the Royal Technical College in Glasgow were men. All the grants under the heading 'miscellaneous' were for men. Two of the places for music and ballet were for men and two for girls, that is two out of 28. In the next year there were 44 grants only three of which were for women. In 1960 of 27 grants, 4 were for women, in 1961 of 21 grants 4 were for women. In 1962 out of 30 grants, 6 were for women.

To be fair to the Cross Trust, this only reflects attitudes within the wider community. There were, in fact, no women applicants for Oxbridge grants until 1960. Women had to learn to aspire. In that year Diane C. Scott, of Girton, an Aberdeen graduate who wanted to be a law publisher, was given a grant of £150. Her lecturer pled her case in words which he knew would appeal: 'Miss Scott has shown her capacity to grow into a forceful personality without losing her natural attractiveness.'

Women studying technological subjects were rare then as now. But Sheena Marr, a graduate in radiography, was helped in 1962 to do Honours Engineering at Aberdeen. The non-educational grants, the outside activities schools, the boys' clubs, did nothing for girls. While men always predominated over women in the lists of grantees this was not so much the policy of the Cross Trustees as the result of the smaller numbers of women being put forward by parents and teachers for further education. But, of course, the means of attracting applicants affected the issue. It had always been the policy of the Trust not to make its existence too widely known so that it should not be flooded with more applications than it would be able to handle or to satisfy. Dr Peddie had been delegated the task of finding and vetting suitable applicants. That he did this very largely by contact with the head-masters of Scottish boys' boarding schools was in itself enough to explain an imbalance which lasted for the next decades. But Dr Peddie was also prone to beliefs which although they could not safely be expressed in public today without condemnation were very generally held then. They were of the kind which suggested that marriage and home making were the first and most important objects for women, that too much study should not be allowed to affect a girl's attractive-ness, that the womanly virtues did not include ambition. All of this went along with geniality and benevolence and would not have attracted a raised eyebrow in his day, but it did mean that women were competing on unequal terms.

Girls had, of course, before ever reaching the Cross Trust, to over-come the prejudice still held by many fathers against further education for girls, especially if there were sons in the family, when it was generally the case that the boys had a prior right.

The original wording of the Cross Trust constitution did not in fact limit help to boys but spoke of 'young men and women'. It was not a legally built-in prohibition which kept down the numbers of young women receiving grants but a received attitude affecting both the Cross Trustees and the wider community. Robin Buchanan Smith, a younger man more in touch with a new generation's thought, spoke up for women, drawing attention to injustice where he saw it, putting it right where it was within his power. He recommended a language student for a grant in 1969, after she had been turned down by another charity, saying: 'It would appear that the Walker Trust have an in-built bias against giving grants for women' and making it plain that he would not care to have the Cross Trust similarly accused.

The founder's own attitudes had been both ambivalent and Victorian. For a man otherwise so kindly and courteous he was remarkably condescending in his attitude to Marjorie Dence, for instance. He had always been generous with help for Perth Repertory Theatre but would have preferred to deal with a male director. In a letter in May 1963 he wrote: 'My dear Peddie, The cuttings are from Glasgow Herald some days ago. The good Marjorie thinks it is a poor picture of her. I don't agree – the look in her face brings to mind the terrible Medusa.' And the language he habitually used to address his house-keeper, who looked after him for many years with efficiency and tolerance, would certainly be thought of today as both unforgivably patronising and inexcusably rude.

Attitudes to women were still unenlightened and the Trustees cannot be blamed for conformity to generally held views. Later in the Eighties, they did, in fact, attempt to right injustices to women when they could. There was the girl born in Scotland of a Pakistani family who wanted to study biochemistry, whose father not only refused to finance her education but, because he believed his daughter's place should be at home, cut her off completely when she left to study in Glasgow. She was assisted with a grant ungrudgingly given. There was an Edinburgh girl living unhappily at home with a father who was a domestic tyrant, who could not adapt himself to the changes in girls' appearance, who made her life a misery because she wore lipstick and mini skirts. She was helped with a grant which allowed her to share a flat with a friend while she attended university. Another girl was helped to escape from a repressive father when her tutor wrote to the Trust begging help on her behalf. 'The student's father is a horrid man and not normal. The home atmosphere is very bad and will be worse henceforth because the father is now about to retire from the Regular Army – he is a Major – and will be more in the house.'

In more recent years the Trustees have shown themselves glad to help young women who applied to them for help in a number of interesting projects. Isobel Janet Cowie, for instance, was helped to make a journey to Australia to study 'a very important modern problem – anorexia nervosa, '... There is no financial hardship except that father has four at university age or nearly so. But the girl's independence and vitality are quite unusual.' It was decided to make her a grant of £300 'for an ambassadress for Scotland who seems to fulfil the intentions of Sir Alexander.'

It was actually easier for the Trustees to help people whose fathers' incomes were too high to be allowed any grant at all from the SED. In that situation the Trust was freed from the worry of risking the withdrawal or reduction of the SED maintenance grant by making a Cross allowance. If the student was getting nothing anyway it could not be taken away and the Trust was left free to help in any way it chose. This perhaps accounts for the help given to such people as High Court judges who might at first sight seem the least needy of beneficiaries.

But they did always help the genuinely needy when they found them. Susan Muir, the daughter of a North Ronaldsay crofter, was given £1,000 a year for two years so that she could go to the Courtauld Institute to study textile conservation. She did not qualify for an SED grant because she already had a degree. This ban on awards of SED grants to graduates was to change the emphasis of grant giving by the Cross Trust, a matter to be treated in a later chapter.

The question of whether or not a woman should give up her career on marriage, of whether or not a husband, however young and financially insecure, should be responsible for supporting a wife, was never completely resolved by the Cross Trust any more than it has been in the rest of society. In the early days, where an ex-serviceman was involved, the Trustees made it possible for a young married couple to travel together by making grants to each of them so that the wife's salary would not be missed when the husband needed to go abroad to complete his studies.

But later on girls who had married during their studies did not have their grants renewed. And men, finding themselves in hard straits because they had married and fathered children were also refused. When McCash and Hunter passed on a request for help with the comment 'Another pathetic letter' it was met with the reply 'Pathetic indeed, but why *do* these chaps get married and have children?'

The blue-stocking, who gave up the idea of marriage for a career, was rewarded but not admired. The 'attractive' girl who put a husband, children, family life before the career was fondly treated but not rewarded.

In the end the Trustees showed themselves, in this as in other things, able to adapt. By 1987 the revised wording used for the SED register of educational endowments made no mention of gender. Its stated purpose was 'to award grants to Scottish graduates, under-graduates or secondary school *pupils*'.

Perhaps the best illustration of the fact that attitudes had changed is that, in 1989, when consideration was given to the question of finding a suitable additional Trustee, they chose Mrs Claire Orr for her wide-ranging administrative experience and her knowledge of the musical world.

The numbers of women helped never quite caught up on the numbers of men but the proportion changed very markedly. In the years 1985–1990, of 166 beneficiaries, 94 were men and 72 women and the women were being helped towards just as diverse a set of opportunities as the men.

As an interesting footnote which illustrates that the Trustees did adjust to changing attitudes, one of their number was, in 1985, in-volved in a case of great importance and interest to women. Lord Fraser (now Lord Fraser of Tullybelton) was one of the three Law Lords who, in the famous appeal of the Department of Health against Victoria Gillick, ruled that doctors were legally entitled to prescribe the contraceptive pill to girls under 16 without parental consent.

Men, of course, also had to conform to a preferred standard. Some of the terms of praise used to describe young men who were taken into the fold of beneficiaries are Edwardian in their terminology and remarkable when it is remembered that the outside world contained brilliant students with long hair, torn jeans and Afghan coats who would emerge from their hippy cocoons to become the respectable professional men of the next decades.

Where the Trustees were ahead of their time was in their kindly and forgiving attitude towards failure and ill health. They were proud of their successes. But it was not necessary to be unfailingly brilliant to win their indulgence. A young man who had been forced to give up his university studies because of what was called 'acute neurosis' was allowed a grant to take a less demanding course elsewhere. Lord Balerno wrote to the Trustees 'I find myself sympathetically inclined – as I always do to anyone who has, so to speak, come "out of the shadows".'

Some approved school boys were helped to buy climbing boots and suitable outdoor clothing for an adventure programme. '£5 per boy seems to me very meagre' wrote Peddie, '£10 seems nearer the mark. The history of these boys is really pretty awful'. Not every Trustee agreed with this grant but it did go through.

On another occasion Lord Balerno recommended backing a boy who had failed his exams through lack of application and who needed a grant to pay for extra tuition. He reminded the Trustees of another beneficiary 'who similarly failed his first year, when we picked him up and put his nose to the grindstone he went on to get a good 2nd and is now doing well with Ferranti.'

And there was the dyslexic boy whose father despaired of him to the point of abandoning him at boarding school, refusing to pay further fees or even his rail fare home. The Cross Trust not only paid his school fees but found holiday accommodation for him, practical farm training when he left school, and paid for him during a lengthy series of operations before he was able to settle into adult life and independence.

A sad story of a boy born out of wedlock to a lady of good family touched their hearts so that they were prepared to pay the boy's school fees anonymously to ensure that no breath about his background should ever reach the boy. Young men from good schools without much in the way of brain were helped with crammers' fees in the often forlorn hope that they might win university entrance that way. Rannoch School, perhaps because of its emphasis on outdoor activities rather than academic competitiveness, began to win a reputation for coping well with dyslexia, a newly fashionable term in the Sixties, and a number of boys were assisted to go there with fees from the Cross Trust.

Sometimes, in fact, one suspects that the Trustees' Christian benevolence was taken advantage of, especially in those cases where a particular child had first caught the attention of the founding chairman and thereafter his whole extended family began to seek ways of extracting grants from the Trust.

Although reports from beneficiaries were insisted upon and high standards of handwriting, grammatical precision and politeness were hoped for, they could be remarkably forgiving about a boy's inability to express gratitude in a decent letter. Lord Balerno begged the Trustees on one boy's behalf 'to overlook this wretched letter.'

In fact it is quite plain that the Cross Trustees, although occasionally differing from each other in degrees of forbearance, although sometimes showing their irritation with the inadequate social behaviour of the young people of the Sixties, were primarily motivated by benevolence and ungrudging in giving help.

Faced with the revolutionary student politics of the 1960s the benevolence of the Trustees must often have been stretched. All over Europe students were occupying administrative buildings, organising street protests and *demos*, marching in solidarity with the workers, some of them patiently and sincerely working towards a better and more equal society, some of them joining in for the excitement and the music and the *sleep-ins*.

The attitude of the Cross Trust towards left-wing politics had been made plain as early as 1948 when a grant was first offered and then withdrawn from one young woman among a group of language students applying for travel courses. Professor Carr, however, shared their views and it was he who had in fact drawn the Trust's attention to the problem she seemed to pose. 'You will appreciate that I cannot discriminate against students because of their political views and I felt that to be fair to the girl I had to give her the chance whilst at the same time I drew your attention to the facts.'

Professor Carr must have known that his drawing attention to the facts would in fact damn her completely. Colonel Spens wrote to Sir Alexander saying 'I do not think politics should come into the question of such grants' and then, apparently without noticing the contradiction, 'except that I personally would consider that no communist should be given a grant to go abroad. If the left wing political societies referred to by Professor Carr are simply labour socialist societies, then certainly I agree a grant should be made.' Britain had at that time, it should be remembered, a Labour Government, so it would have been difficult to outlaw student Labour societies, 'but if they are communist societies' he went on 'I do think the point has come where a line should be drawn. I should add that David feels the same as I do.'

The grant had been recorded as passed in the minutes of the last meeting. Cross replied to Spens 'Sheila Baird is very definitely a communist. I think the best way will be for you to kindly redraw the Minute making a grant to the 2 other St A. students and omitting Sheila Baird.'

The Trustees' views simply reflect the received opinion of their day. After the end of the wartime alliance with Soviet Russia, Sir Winston Churchill had fanned the fear of a communist take-over of all Europe, the United States was in the grip of hysterical anxiety about communist inspired anti-American activities and the very word *communist* was associated with treason and danger. It was hardly to be expected that in such a climate the Trustees could look charitably upon a communist student leader.

In later years political opinions are never again overtly referred to. It is only occasionally when a particular name rings a bell from the newspaper reports of student disturbances that the reader understands why 'Dr Peddie reported on this student and it was resolved to make no further grant to him.' Although this particular student had been a beneficiary throughout school and a brilliant career at Cambridge his noisy participation in subversive student politics was enough to exclude him from further grants for study abroad.

The disturbances at Stirling University in the 60s, and when the Queen's visit was marred by noisy demonstrations by the preponderantly left-wing students of this then very new foundation, caused a good deal of distress and applications from that source for grants were not thereafter encouraged.

Newspaper reports and television broadcasts from the Paris of 1968 were invigorating and exciting for the young but alarming for those of conventional outlook. The Cross Trust carried on its work during this period with a calm attentiveness towards the job in hand only rarely diverted from their generally benevolent attitude towards young people, their needs, their aspirations and their failings.

7

THE SEVENTIES

As we have seen, certain important changes in the administration of the nation's educational system affected the affairs of the Cross Trust during the Sixties. The insistence that charitable endowments concerned with education should in important ways be made accountable to the SED to some extent limited what it was possible to do. It also made some former activities seem less worthwhile. The Trustees had carried out a review of what avenues were left open to them and came to certain conclusions. For instance it was minuted that 'a condition of future grants should be that the student be required to apply for an allowance through the usual channels and that any award from the Trust be deferred until the amount of the allowance had been ascertained.' There had been administrative difficulties in making grants to students which later had either to be withdrawn or augmented when the SED made unexpected decisions.

They were also affected by government policy towards the Arts and in particular by the 'recently announced policy on the part of the Chancellor of the Exchequer to make available a considerable sum of money in support of the Repertory movement in Great Britain and on the understanding that the Arts Council of Great Britain was charged with the duty of ascertaining the financial position of each company . . . it was agreed that, meantime, no assistance from the Trust should be made to Scottish Repertory Theatres.' The Chairman undertook to notify Miss Dence and the Gateway Theatre was informed that their application 'was of a nature that ought properly to be met by the Home Board and not by the Trust.'

This ruling was not strictly adhered to and when it turned out that Arts Council funds would never be lavish enough to support all the needs of the theatre the long-standing beneficiaries of the Trust, Perth Repertory Theatre, the Byre in St Andrews and the Gateway in Edinburgh continued to derive intermittent support.

Travel grants for language students and research grants for scientists should continue to be made and it was agreed 'it would be reasonable to award part of the Trust funds to students proceeding to public schools where the government gives no assistance or only minor assistance.' The question of whether the payment of boarding school fees was strictly within the letter of the Constitution was one which arose from time to time and the resolution in the Sixties affected Trust policy for a number of years.

The other resolution taken at this time was that there would be no blank cheques for charitable bodies or institutions or schools requiring assistance in a general way. Particular projects might or might not win approval and financial help but that help would only be forthcoming when the project had actually been completed. Funds would not in future be put into the hands of the National Trust or any similar body for them to use or not use as they chose. They must be allocated for a named and necessary expenditure.

Restrictions of this kind were enforced by uneasiness about the ready availability of income to cover all the growing demands made upon the Trust. During the lifetime of Sir Alexander Cross he had personally controlled the investment policy of the Trust, taking an interest in it exactly as he had done when the money had been part of his own personal capital. With the help of his stockbrokers and of the staff of McCash and Hunter, he had pursued a knowledgeable and successful campaign of buying and selling shares with the effect of producing sufficient income to fulfil the grant-giving policy of his Trust.

On his death the Trustees set up a Finance Committee to keep an eye on investments, consisting only of Lord Keith and Mr David Murray, because, as Keith said, in financial matters the smaller the committee the more effective. However Lord Keith himself died shortly thereafter and the frequent absence of Lord Fraser meant that more and more responsibility for financial matters had to be put upon the Trust's professional advisers and in particular Mr James Ross of McCash and Hunter, whose worth to the Trust was recognised when, at the end of this decade, he was assumed as a trustee.

Inflation had begun to be noticeable during the 1960s. In 1962 it was reported that 'Prices in London are now such that it is extremely difficult to live there under £500 a year.' There was some pressure, moved by a general desire on the part of the Trustees not to seem niggardly, to raise the level of grants to keep pace with rising costs to students. They preferred to limit the number of grants so that they could afford to be generous to those they did accept as grantees.

Another sign of rising inflation was the abandonment of the flat rate of 10 guineas for Trustees' expenses 'because expenses vary widely and it was thought that individual applications for expenses should be made.'

By 1969 it was resolved that investment policy should be framed so as to ensure a minimum gross annual income of £32,000. At the beginning of that decade a sum of £13,000 had been sufficient. By 1975, only half way through the decade, the sum was £34,000 and continuing to rise.

In 1971 the advice from the stockbrokers warned of 'fear of a general falling off in world trade. There seemed to be too many question marks to justify much action by a charitable fund.' A number of institutions were made grants, for instance of £500 to Edinburgh Youth Orchestra and £1,000 to Scottish Opera, on the strict understanding that these were not to be recurring grants and that they must be anonymous. The Trust had learned to be wary of being ensnared by annual appeals from bodies to which they had once yielded sympathy, and made it their policy henceforth to avoid recurring grants. There was a danger of finding themselves with a burden of annual commitments which left little scope for new awards to perhaps more deserving cases.

They were still keen to comply with the wishes of the founder and to give the little extra that made it possible for a student to derive real benefit from his studies. For the first few years of the Seventies they were circumscribed by a temporary insufficiency of funds but by April 1972 the Finance Committee were noting with satisfaction the considerable rise in the value of investments. Some new consideration had to be given to the best way of spreading investment. 'There was no power to invest in Europe and this would have to be done by investing in Companies with interests on that Continent.' This restriction must presumably have been a hangover from the wartime conditions prevailing at the time of the Trust's foundation when the continent of Europe was cut off by Nazi occupation. After some deliberation it was ruled that investment in Hong Kong need not be similarly limited by the Constitution.

Having a little more money at their disposal the Trustees found it possible and gratifying to be generous during this period. So a Rotary scholar was given an extra £300 'to allow him to travel more widely in America than his scholarship permits.' Neil Mackie, completing postgraduate studies at the College of Music in London, with a grant of £250, was given a further £250 to make his début in the Wigmore Hall and, in addition to £400 from the Munster Trust, he was granted an extra £400 because the Trustees had discovered that Mackie's mother was seriously ill in Aberdeen and travelling from London to visit her was straining his resources. Alastair Taylor, ex-President of Glasgow University Union, had graduated and obtained a job demonstrating computers, but as this involved a great deal of travelling the Trustees granted him £500 to buy a car.

This was one step too far in generosity and the next report from the auditors, Coopers and Lybrand, in September 1973, remarked that 'included in the awards and grants under Schedule A is a payment to a former student to assist him to purchase a car which was necessary for his work as a trainee representative. The trustees may wish to consider whether this payment is in accordance with the Trust Deed.' In less closely-examined times cars had been allowed to students when the Trustees thought they would bring real benefit. One botanist, wandering widely in search of specimens, and one painter, travelling Europe with easel and canvases, had already had cars purchased for them. But the climate of political opinion and the increased vigilance of Inland Revenue officers meant that any grants awarded must be strictly within the powers given to the Trustees by their constitution. Cars were not offered thereafter but the Trust still proclaimed that 'Our policy is that if we make a grant at all it should not be cut to the bone.'

That perhaps some recent applicants had been less worthy than was hoped is suggested by a minute of a meeting at which 'the Chairman spoke of the correspondence that had passed between the Trust and the SED and it was resolved that in future consideration would only be given to cases where there was a reputable individual sponsor personally known to one or more of the Trustees.'

There was plenty of scope left, and some very interesting individual ventures were backed by the Trustees during the Seventies. The Maclaren of Maclaren 'whose family is fairly poor' and who had already been helped with a kitting out grant, was given £200 to go to America during his long vacation in order to obtain information to enable him to write a social historical essay on the origins of the Maclaren families.

Another student was given £235 to go to Memphis to study fish farming. 'There is little doubt' wrote Lord Balerno 'that Fish Farming is a growth industry and some forecast that by 1990 half the fish eaten in Britain will be cultivated, not hunted. I think this would be a good start in life for James.' As far as salmon goes, Lord Balerno has been proved right.

Owen Murray was allowed £600 to study classical accordion at the Royal Danish Music Conservatory, 'but it was made very clear to him that this was for one year only and no extension would be granted.' A Royal College of Music student, Peter Sanders, was made a grant of £350 with which to buy an oboe. The violin bought earlier for Daphne Godson was now valued for insurance purposes at £7,000 which caused some deliberation about who should be responsible for paying the rather hefty insurance charges.

Music had always been one of Sir Alexander Cross's first priorities. Although it was not at first found easy to interpret his wishes, in these later years many individual music students were helped in addition to the grants made to a number of orchestras.

Another interesting project was the workshop built for Hamish McInnes under the wing of the National Trust in which it was planned that he would produce mountain safety equipment. A second plea for help by McInnes was later refused.

As well as helping individuals the Trust continued during the Seventies the policy of helping boys' clubs and outdoor centres, particularly those in which one or other of the Trustees had a special interest.

There seems to shine through the minutes of the Seventies an eagerness to fulfil the founder's wishes about the encouragement of healthy pursuits and outdoor activities for boys. Lord Balerno and his son did their best to find and encourage ventures which seemed to them to embody the ideal of widening horizons while at the same time sheltering from trouble boys at the awkward adolescent stage. The 1961 resolution had emphasized that 'Boys' Clubs, the Moray Sea School and the Outward Bound Trust were excellent bodies for this Trust to support.' While Sir Alexander Cross had, for the most part, given his attention and help to middle class boys at boarding school, the Buchanan Smiths extended the range of help towards less privileged youths. One particular project was the Currie Kirk Youth Club which Alick Buchanan Smith was instrumental in founding, for which he organised grants and in which he continued to take an interest even when his time became more and more stretched.

The Currie Club was founded on ideals straight from John Buchan. The members were formed into groups known as Reivers, the 14 and

15 year olds, and Callants, the 16 year olds, and apprentice Reivers, 12 and 13 year olds. They spent their evenings at football training, gymnastics and woodwork, with Bible Class on Sundays, Duke of Edinburgh Award and Red Cross training on Mondays, something for every night but Friday. The Callants found evening attendance difficult 'because of other work commitments' but the Club seems to have been popular with the younger age groups. 'At present' the Trust was told 'much depends on Alick's personal supervision and planning for the future and parliamentary duties would of course greatly limit the time he would have available but as the Club is his own creation he will maintain an interest in it.'

The Club was helped throughout the Sixties and other awards were made thereafter, £1,500 in 1972 and £1,000 in 1975 when it was said to be going from strength to strength.

Robin Buchanan Smith, although employed as chaplain to St Andrews University and often of help to needy students there, spent free time when he could on the west coast of Scotland and was a believer in the benefits of hard open-air exercise. He looked for and discovered there projects which seemed to him worth rewarding with grants. One of them was the Project Trust, on the Isle of Coll. This was a kind of adventure school which had first contacted the Trust in 1971 with a request for assistance from an address in London. The Trustees decided then that 'it did not come within the Constitution of this Trust'. In 1974, however, Mr Buchanan Smith 'had made further enquiries about the Trust, had visited Coll and made extensive investigations.' It was found possible to help individual boys and girls taking part in the Project Trust's activities, even if the institution itself was not to be allowed a grant. The sum of £500 was put aside to assist volunteers recommended by the Project Trust but when three names were put forward the sum was raised to £750 to provide each participant with £250. As a general rule, schemes which got young people out and about were likely to be looked on with favour and the Reverend Selby Wright's Boys' Club Camp at Skateraw near Dunbar was another beneficiary. The Reverend Selby Wright had been helped early in the history of the Cross Trust in his capacity as a crammer, when he took boys who had failed their public school exams into his house as lodgers and prepared them for resits. Another project was the Livingstone Youth Trust which sought assistance in 1975 to send six boys to Loch Eil for three weeks. £300 was contributed towards their costs.

There were still many applications for grants from families finding boarding school fees a burden. Now, though, the reasons for needing help had changed. Where once it was a widowed mother who asked for assistance now it was very likely to be a father whose business had failed in the climate of declining trade, or one who had been made redundant by a company in which he had thought himself safe. Economic conditions are reflected in the grant applications received by the Cross Trust as is the change in social patterns which showed itself in more frequent marital breakdowns.

It became, at the same time, more and more necessary to discriminate. Far more applications are turned down during this period and the Trustees, becoming aware perhaps of the need to be objective in their judgment, tried to rationalise their reasons for rejection. As before they prefer to continue to support former beneficiaries whose worthiness and gratitude have been proved and are chary about taking on new commitments, but they are careful to obtain continuing reports about each of them. Those whose fathers' circumstances have improved are expected to confess that fact and to have their grants reduced. Those who fail to report on their progress do not have grants renewed for another year. Where one of the Trustees has investigated a case and found a family's financial position to be less circumscribed than had been reported a grant is refused. Applications from students who have changed subjects and seek grants for a second degree are usually, though not invariably, refused. Students who have failed a year at university and have therefore forfeited their SED allowance, are not helped by the Trust. And, as well as these refusals of individual applications, bodies and institutions making appeals are very rigorously examined from now on. There is a very evident dislike of 'appeal literature' and professional fund-raisers and a clear intention never to give funds for any vaguely defined objective but only for properly described and limited projects. Edinburgh University Students Association was one of those refused. 'The Trustees were not attracted to the subject matter of the appeal nor to the fact that it was being conducted by professional fund raisers and it was decided to give no assistance.'

What becomes apparent is a gradual change in the circumstances of applicants, a change which was to become very marked during the next decade.

8

THE EIGHTIES

The young people applying for grants in the Fifties and Sixties, the young people Captain Cross had in mind when he first formed his Trust, seem in retrospect very unworldly compared with the new kind of applicant appearing first in the Seventies and becoming predominant in the Eighties: ambitious, mature men and women on their way to significant careers and exploring efficiently every means of raising funds to help their progress.

Among them are many lawyers and medical students looking for grants which will help them to take steps towards professional qualifications. They are all well aware that, in the push for jobs, degree passes are no longer enough. They have to prove that they have travelled extensively. A fortnight's trip to Paris is not now enough to prove that their minds have been broadened. They have to go to Papua New Guinea, Mexico, Tasmania, Africa, very often as volunteers in some charitable or research project. They are no older than their counterparts of the Fifties but they are remarkably wiser, smarter, less diffident and they are extremely good at form-filling, at presenting themselves, at making out a good case for help. There are, of course, immeasurably more projects for them to take part in and a wide open world for them to move about in.

Dr Peddie's certainties were sorely missed. He had died in 1979 when this appreciation was recorded in the minutes: 'He was one of the founder members of the Trust and one of the dominant factors of the success of the Trust's policy. He had given valiant service to the Trust and to the young men and women who benefited from it and in particular those of musical talent. It was feared it would be difficult if not impossible to find a suitable replacement for him.' As if to emphasize this two further appointments were made to the Trust at this time, Mr James Ross, of McCash and Hunter, who had served for many years as Secretary Treasurer to the Trust and Dr Anthony Ritchie, Dr Peddie's second successor as Secretary to the Carnegie Trust for the Universities of Scotland.

The first Chairman had died in 1963, his friend and adviser Lord Keith the year after. Colonel Hugh Spens of Maclay Murray and Spens, the Cross family lawyers, had died in 1959. Now, with Dr Peddie's death, four out of the five original Trustees were gone. Mr David Murray, not among the original Trustees but appointed in 1946, very shortly after the foundation, chose to retire in 1982.

Although not party to the making of the Trust's formative policies, it was the loss of Lord Balerno in 1984 which in fact brought to an end the Cross Trust in the form in which it had been born. As Sir Alick Buchanan Smith he had been appointed only after the first death among the original Trustees, in 1956, but it was he who was closest to the philosophy of Sir Alexander Cross, knowing him, indeed, only as an elderly man but becoming his friend and confidant, trusted to carry on his creation in accordance with his own hopes and wishes and sharing to a large extent his outlook on life. When, in 1989, Lord Fraser of Tullybelton, Sir Alexander's cousin, died, the last link with the original Trust disappeared. Lord Fraser had been chairman from 1984–1989.

The Reverend the Hon. Robin Buchanan Smith, of course, had known Sir Alexander and in fact introduced his father to him and he proved to be the natural successor to a tradition of benevolent paternalism. But he was a young man when first appointed and in fact his appointment, in 1959, should be seen as a demonstration of the willingness of the other Trustees to understand and respect the viewpoint of the young. He was fitted to take the Trust into the difficult times of its fifth decade in a way that would have been hard for older men. Being younger he was flexible and able to recognise modern trends without deploring them. Most of all he was able to accept that the Trust must necessarily be limited in future in what it could do and that it would have to learn to select from the overwhelming number of new applicants those to whom it could be of most benefit. There were confusing times ahead and for a while it seemed as if the Trustees had lost the confident certainty about the best way forward which they had once shared. The country was undergoing a radical shake-up which was plunging trade into recession, industry into decline and education into a state of confusion. This state of affairs is reflected both in the volume of applications for help and in their diversity. There are no grandees among the Trustees now, no QCs, no peerages, no large fortunes. These are professional people, with lives outside the Cross Trust, giving it their time and interest, but perhaps bringing a breadth of more ordinary experience than the original Trustees had known. None of the new Trustees had been involved with framing the original constitution. If they had known the founder at all they had known him only as an elderly man. They were freer, in a way, to interpret his wishes to suit the demands of modern society, but in other ways they were far less free than he had been because of the limitations put upon them by government.

In 1990 Mr James Ross of McCash and Hunter retired from the Trust. The Trustees, in minuting their regret, used words from a letter written almost forty years ago by Sir Alexander Cross: 'Ross is very able, completely reliable and I find invaluable; he never spares himself trouble, and there's nothing about the Cross Trust, and our grantees, with which he is not completely familiar.'

His retiral meant that there were now only three Trustees left, the Reverend R.D. Buchanan Smith, Mrs Claire Orr and Dr A.E. Ritchie. At the meeting of 23 August 1990, held in the Carnegie Trust offices in Edinburgh they agreed that suitable additional Trustees should be sought. As a result of some thoughtful research Mr Dougal Philip was appointed in November 1990 and Dr Roy MacGregor in February 1991. In recognition of the fact that he was carrying the work previously handled by Mr Ross, Mr Mark Webster of McCash and Hunter was appointed as Trustee in November 1993.

There was now a full complement of Trustees to meet the increased work-load of applicants which fell to be considered both as a result of the increasing public availability of the Trust's constitution and as a consequence of government policy on grant giving. Even with extra hands the burden of giving fair attention to each of the many applicants grew heavier and heavier. In February 1992 it was decided that it should no longer be necessary for every Trustee to see the papers for every applicant. Instead each Trustee was given authority to refuse an application he or she felt certain was unsuitable without first consulting the other Trustees. And where an applicant seemed worthy of an award one Trustee on his own could authorise that award, so long as it fell under £1,000 and was passed to the Chairman for ratification. This both speeded up business and avoided administrative trouble. Something could be achieved between meetings without lengthy correspondence and difficulties about arranging contact between Trustees.

One of the causes of the increase in the volume of applications was the very high number of 'medical electives' seeking funding for foreign travel. Medical students in their final years were expected to spend some time in practical work in their chosen field of study. Although this could be done in Britain, indeed could be done within their own universities, students felt that career chances would be enhanced by experience in more exotic or even dangerous parts of the world. So they sought funds to go to very faraway places which were both expensive to reach and unable to support them. The Trust could help only a small proportion of them. The problem was that every one of these young people was clever, adventurous, worthy of help. Choosing between them became increasingly difficult and there was some feeling among the Trustees that the press of medical elective applicants was squeezing out students of the Arts and Sciences. In the autumn of 1992 it was decided that medical students looking for support for study abroad would henceforth have to compete for places. There were to be no more than 20 grantees in this category, applications would have to be lodged by April of each year so that they could be considered together and the advice of expert assessors would be sought.

Social changes with legislative consequences also had their effects on the interpretation of the Constitution. On two separate occasions the Trustees requested that the Opinion of Counsel be obtained to check that the current interpretation by the Trustees of the requirement that all applicants must be of 'Scottish Birth or Parentage' was correct. On the first occasion in 1967 in an Opinion given by Mr H.S. Keith, QC, the advice given was that the position of the mother of an applicant should be disregarded. The circumstances had, however, altered by 1988 when a further Opinion was obtained, this time from J.A.S. Hope, QC, now Lord Hope, in which it was made clear that it would be inconsistent with changes which had occurred in the law to continue to take that view and that the modern trend towards equality of husband and wife in every respect required an alteration of approach whereby regard should be had equally to both parents so that if either the father or mother of an applicant was Scottish then the applicant would be eligible for consideration as a beneficiary.

In the early days applications for grants had been made by letter to the Cross Trust. Sir Alexander particularly liked to judge an applicant's handwriting and his ability to express himself politely. But because this often necessitated a follow-up correspondence to obtain answers to questions not raised in the original letter, it was decided to have printed a form of application which would require answers to all the questions the Trustees needed to put. In the late 1970s a request for a passport photograph was added and on several occasions, most recently in 1989, new application forms were drafted, each time more strictly defining the guidelines in answer to the increasing flow of applications.

During what have come to be known as the Thatcher years, government's increasing reluctance to fund social projects put increased pressure on charitable trusts both from individual students finding it difficult to find funds elsewhere and from institutions which had once enjoyed government backing for their activities. Charities in general have traditionally avoided long term social commitments from which they might not be able to escape. That is why the Cross Trust chose not to give lump sums to Strathclyde University, for instance, or the National Trust or the Project Trust but preferred to consider applications from individual students or for individual projects. All charitable trusts recoiled from what seemed in the Eighties to be a growing demand to provide not one-off contributions for special needs but core funding for bodies which might come to be wholly dependent upon them. Not unpredictably, they did not welcome reports which claimed that, as trusts were now playing a more and more important role in society they should be monitored more closely: 'They have the privilege of not paying any income tax,' said one writer 'and yet they decide themselves where their funds are allocated.' It was disturbing that the malpractice discovered in English charities should cast suspicion upon the very differently managed Scottish trusts. And it seemed particularly unfair to most of those involved in the administration of charitable trusts that government should itself seek to step back from social responsibilities and yet at the same time demand a say in the way charitable grants were to be allocated.

Interference remained limited to a more rigorous application of guidelines about income tax liability and to demands for publication of constitutions and purposes. The SED had already, as we have seen, demanded information from all educational charities about their constitutions and the extent of their grant-giving and had drawn up a list of trusts involved in education. It was a useful tool for the SED and resulted in a flood of applicants to the Cross Trust from students who had received information about the Trust from the SED. The Trustees were therefore well aware that any further publicity would result in a greatly increased number of applicants and they were anxious so to define their purposes as to limit the number as far as they could within the terms of their constitution. The result was to boil down the pages of the constitution's grant-giving policy to the one entry: 'To award Scholarships and grants to Scottish graduates, undergraduates or secondary school pupils or to promote studies of Scottish Natural History or to assist the performance of drama and opera and to support bodies which promote these objects.'

In 1985 the Scottish Council for Community and Voluntary Organisations requested from the Cross Trust information for inclusion in a Directory of Grant Making Trusts in Scotland. It was agreed at that stage that details of the Trust should not be provided but the Trustees understood that they would eventually be forced to concede and Dr Ritchie undertook to ascertain whether there was a more suitable Register in which details could be given. At the next meeting Dr Ritchie reported that he had received, completed and returned a questionnaire with information about the Cross Trust which would appear in the Grants Register for 1987/89. The Secretaries were requested to write to the SED to request that the details held on their Register of Educational endowments should conform to the information which had been submitted for inclusion in the Grants Register.

They had to abandon, in the face of this new requirement to register, their habit of anonymity and in 1985 it was minuted that 'The current policy that successful applicants should not tell others about this Trust was considered and it was decided that this policy should no longer apply. To show that the policy was only reluctantly abandoned, however, 'The Secretaries were instructed not to mention this to future successful applicants.' This represented, of course, no real change. Favoured beneficiaries had always been trusted to pass on information about the Trust within restricted circles. It was only in more doubtfully acceptable circles that anonymity was insisted upon.

In 1990 Parliament passed the Law Reform (Miscellaneous Provisions) (Scotland) Act, giving government much wider powers over the conduct of charities in Scotland. Mr Webster drew up for the Cross Trust a paper describing the Act's principal provisions and their expected effect.

The most important provision was the power given to the Inland Revenue to disclose 'to any person who requests it' the name and address of any Scottish charity and the corresponding power given to the Lord Advocate to interdict any charity found to be improperly managed.

The Act also made it obligatory for a charity to provide a copy of its Constitution and Accounts to anyone who should request it on payment of a reasonable charge to cover copying and postage. Clearly, there was the prospect that many more members of the public would find out about the Trust and in order to ensure so far as possible that information readily available to the public was correct and in the hope of avoiding unsuitable applications, a new entry for the S.C.V.O. Charities Questionnaire was devised in March 1993. Its wording was as follows:

> Individuals must be young people of Scottish birth or parentage; awards are intended to extend the boundaries of human life.
> The Trustees have discretion in making such awards and are prepared to consider support for short term educational studies. Applicants will be required to have a record of distinction and ability and to put forward proposals for study or undertakings which are of demonstrable merit. Such proposals may be in any recognised discipline, including the visual and performing arts, and music.
> Awards will in all cases be made having regard to the degree of financial hardship which the study or project may devolve on the applicant or his or her family.
> Limited funds are available to charitable bodies currently known to the Trustees.

This, while referring carefully to the aims and intentions of the founder, protects the Trust in important ways. First, it requires excellence. Sir Alexander Cross had perhaps imagined his money helping young people towards distinction. Half a century later distinction is required of them before they can even aspire to become applicants. This is underlined in the minute of 16 November 1993 when the Chairman said: 'The Trustees always had to bear in mind that they were not in the business of helping lame ducks.'

Secondly, new applications from organisations not already supported by the Trust, have been effectively excluded by the wording of this entry. The Trustees seem to have agreed to put individuals first when sharing out the money available to them, while at the same time not abandoning those institutions with whom they had had a long association. Their continued support for the SYHA, for instance, has been marked by a significant award of £20,000 which was 'considered appropriate on the 50th anniversary of the founding of the Trust, in particular in view of the keen interest of the Founder in the work of the Association.'

The need to publish forced the Trustees into serious thinking about the way in which their responsibilities should be undertaken and the way in which the wishes of the founder should be interpreted and in fact this reappraisal was in the long run of benefit to them. The minutes give the impression that, after a period of inconsistency and doubt, the new Trustees move forward into the Nineties, and towards the end of the Trust's half century, with new certainties and determination.

Everything has become brisker than in the early days of the Trust; no long weekend gatherings at Battleby, only short businesslike meetings on office premises. There is no one left for whom the Trust is the centre of his life, as it became for Sir Alexander Cross. The Trustees are now busy people for whom the Trust is an acceptable responsibility, a real interest, but only one part of their lives. It does not suffer for that. It is just as well administered and perhaps more fairly and rationally, if one can talk in those terms, by these emotionally uninvolved people as by its intensely paternalistic founder.

The minute books, however, are inevitably less interesting without the little notes which passed in such profusion between the first two chairmen and their co-Trustees. Those notes convey still so much of the genuine warmth, real benevolence, Christian charity, humour, irritability, tolerance and exasperation of the founder and his first successor. Without them one knows less of the thinking which led to acceptance or rejection of claims: but, certainly in the last decade, the Trustees had to become inured to saying no and just as certainly they were as generously disposed as circumstances allowed towards those they let through the dock gates into the harbour of Cross protection.

Some very interesting projects have been funded in recent years. In 1985 three Aberdeen students setting off to cycle 19,000 miles in 12 months, from the southern tip of South America to Alaska, on a fund-raising trip on behalf of Tenovus, were each awarded £500. The salary of a tutor for the Scottish Field Studies Centre at Kindrogan, near Kirkmichael was paid for one year. A young woman was granted a travel award to study the reproductive biology of small New World monkeys. The tendency seems to have been to award fewer, but much larger, grants, £2,700 for a drama student, £5,250 for a student at the National Opera School, £2,000 for a violin for a postgraduate music student, £5,000 for hostel refurbishment for the Scottish Schoolboys

Club. A young woman who joined the National Expedition to the Kluane Wilderness in the Yukon was awarded £1,000. There are indications about changed priorities in the wider world. A student was granted £1,000 for in-service training with the Commission of European Communities in Brussels, and £5,000 for each of three years was awarded to support Youth Environmental Education in Europe under the Youth Conservation Exchange Scheme. A law student was awarded £1,200 to allow him to study policing in Hong Kong.

These are all schemes which would probably not have attracted SED funding. It would appear that the Cross Trust, in common with larger charities, conducted a policy of not replacing grants which have been cut from the public sector in government cost-cutting exercises but preferred to support projects which would always have had difficulty getting funding from elsewhere. When new forms were printed, yet again, in 1988/89, in particular to set guidelines which would be appropriate for applicants already holding a first degree, the result was an increased number of refusals, mostly because the applicants were already receiving SED grants. In Dr Peddie's day the holding of an SED grant was almost a prerequisite for receiving a Cross Trust grant, it being accepted by the Trustees that an SED grant required supplementing to allow a civilised standard of living. That generous habit had to be abandoned. Now the problem was to ensure that some students did not become so practised at acquiring grants that they obtained awards from several charitable trusts at once, leaving others less skilful without any help at all. To avoid this, the Trustees considered exchanging information with other educational trusts 'to ensure that funds which were allocated to students were properly used.' No formal steps were taken at this time but the Trustees were becoming more and more cautious in their scrutiny of applications.

A student who wanted to take a course in Naturopathy was, not unsurprisingly, refused as was the Bristol Old Vic Theatre School student who asked for £18,500. Young people seeking funds to join Operation Raleigh were also in general refused, perhaps because the Cross Trust did not wish to be confused with commercial sponsors. A number of medical students who had previously received grants were asked to fill out the new application forms and were afterwards refused further awards. It is very evident that many university students, finding help with fees and maintenance no longer forthcoming under the new restricted government educational policy, are turning to charitable institutions for help and that charities are signalling to government their reluctance, indeed their inability, to take up the burden. They would help in very special cases. For instance, a man who had failed to earn the necessary minimum salary which would entitle him to a mature student grant because he had been nursing a wife dying of cancer, was given a small award.

It remained easier to get a grant for the study of bats or monkeys than for film animation or printed textiles but this could be taken as a reflection of the wishes of the founder who had included the study of natural history among the subjects to be encouraged in his constitution.

In fact, it would seem that at the end of its first half century the Cross Trust had pursued the aims of its founder in a way that would not have displeased him in the face of changes in society which he could hardly have envisaged.

APPENDICES

APPENDIX 1

THE CROSS TRUST
TOTALS OF PAYMENTS TO BENEFICIARIES

Ten year period	Individuals	Scottish Youth Clubs or Associations which promote a love of nature and Scottish scenery	Promotion of drama, opera and similar works
1943–1954	£38,950.00	£9,575.00	£7,383.21
1955–1963	£90,121.28	£3,472.00	£9,490.75
1964–1973	£182,897.79	£18,045.00	£12,400.00
1974–1984	£266,397.66	£13,000.00	£17,670.00
1985–1994	£812,541.00	£106,665.00	£40,215.00
Totals	**£1,390,907.73**	**£150,757.00**	**£87,158.96**

APPENDIX 2

THE CROSS TRUST
LIST OF TRUSTEES FROM 1943–1993

Sir Alexander Cross, Hon. LL D	1943–1963
The Hon. Ian Lord Fraser of Tullybelton, PC	1943–1989
The Hon. James Lord Keith of Avonholm, PC, Hon. LL D	1943–1964
Dr John R. Peddie, CBE, DL, FRSE, FEIS, Hon. LL D	1943–1979
Col. Hugh B. Spens, CBE, DSO, DL	1943–1958
Mr David Murray	1946–1982
The Hon. Alick Lord Balerno, CBE, TD, DL, FRSE, FRSGS	1956–1984
The Rev. the Hon. Robin D. Buchanan Smith	1959–
Mr James Ross	1980–1990
Dr Anthony E. Ritchie, CBE, Hon. LL D, FRSE	1980–
Mrs Claire Orr	1989–
Mr Dougal R.G. Philip	1990–
Dr A. Roy MacGregor	1991–
Mr Mark Webster	1993–

INDEX